LONGMAN GROUP LIMITED
Harlow, Essex
Associated companies, branches
and representatives throughout
the world

First published 1982

Designed and produced by
Grisewood & Dempsey Ltd.

Printed in Italy by Vallardi
Industrie Grafiche, Milan

Wicks, Keith
Sound and recording – (Understanding science)
1. Sound-recording and reproducing – Juvenile literature
I. Title II. Paton, John III. Series
621.389.32 TK7881.4

ISBN 0-582-39169-5

UNDERSTANDING SCIENCE

Sound and Recording

Longman

CONTENTS

Author
Keith Wicks

Editor
John Paton

FOREWORD

Our sense of hearing seems to be an essential part of a full life. Without it we find it difficult to communicate with our fellow human beings, to pass on our knowledge to other people, to listen to a Beethoven symphony or jump at the blare of a motor horn.

This book covers the world of sound in which we live. It describes the physical nature of sound and explains how the ear and brain translate air vibrations into speech, music and plain noise.

In non-technical words and pictures it deals with acoustics, sound studios, tape recording, stereo and hi-fi, and introduces the reader to amplifiers and loudspeakers, records and domestic sound systems.

In the area of music, the author discusses the frequency range of instruments, harmonics and the quality of sound – chords, discords and electronic sound. He also takes a look into the future in the fields of speech and music synthesis, speaking machines and electronic speech recognition.

Everyday Sounds

Sounds can soothe or stimulate; they can also cause us permanent injury. And, while some sounds may distract our attention, others give us information. Sirens can warn of impending danger, or tell factory workers when it is time to go home. And church bells summon the faithful to their services. All these sounds are simple signals. Army buglers blare out more complex signals, transmitting various messages by playing musical phrases.

Orchestral music is an extremely complex mixture of sounds, often designed by the composer to put us in a particular mood. Bright, lively music can cheer us up, while slower, softer music can make us sad. Music is thus a language of sound, by which the composer can communicate with others.

Speech

Many animals communicate by means of sound. A common example is the use of a loud warning signal to indicate the presence of an enemy, or some other danger. Other signals, such as birdsong, are much more complicated. But none of them matches the complexity of human speech. Once, the only sounds people could make were grunts, yells and other simple sounds. Then, over tens of thousands of years, they learned to do more things; they introduced more sounds to describe new activities. The number of basic sounds they could make was fairly limited. So they had to make up words from various combinations of sounds in order to expand their vocabulary. In this way, recognizable languages slowly developed.

Speech Variations

Besides conveying a particular message to us, speech can also tell us something about the person who is talking. People living in different regions of a country usually speak the same language, but with a different accent. The most common differences occur in the pronunciation of vowel sounds. These and other speech differences would enable almost any English-speaking person to distinguish between a Londoner and someone from the North of England or a New Yorker and someone from the Southern states. And an expert can often pinpoint the city from which a person comes, just by hearing him speak. For, within each region, there are local variations in accent and in the words and expressions used. The result is that quite small areas have their own language variety, or dialect. Throughout a person's life, his accent can change considerably. At school, he may be taught how to improve the way he speaks. And, at university or at work, he may gradually acquire the accent of those around him. However, some traces of his original accent usually remain.

Although people from the same place tend to speak in a similar way, there are still detectable differences in their voices. An obvious kind of difference is that some people speak in a deep, low-pitched voice, while others have a high-pitched, sometimes harsh quality. But even people who sound alike have voice differences that can be detected electronically. The sounds they make can be printed as graphs called

The disc record reproducer is almost a hundred years old. During that time gigantic strides have been made in the quality of sound available in our homes. The much-enlarged photograph on the left shows a modern diamond stylus on a sapphire arm. In the background can be seen the grooves in a 33 rpm stereo record.

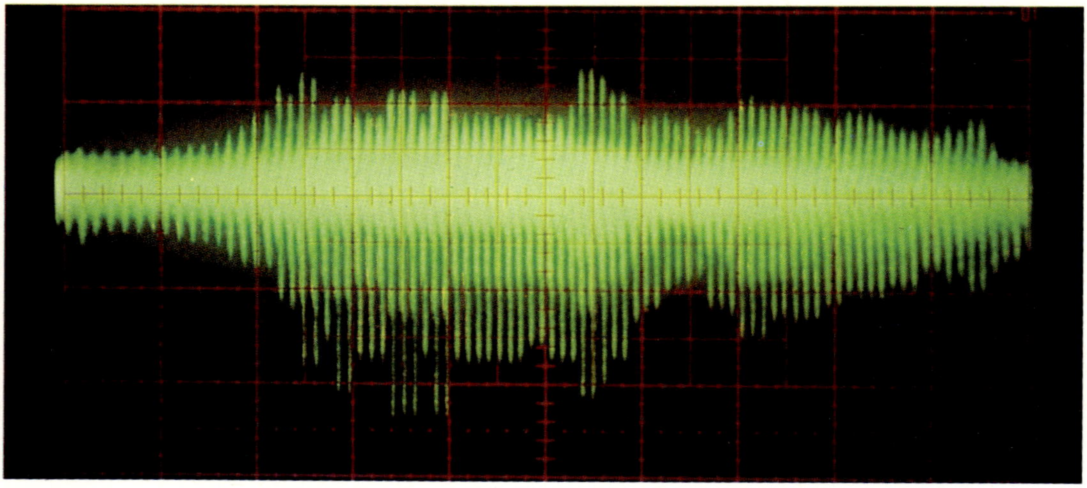

voiceprints. As with fingerprints, each person produces a different pattern. So a voiceprint can often be used to identify a person, simply from the sound he makes when speaking.

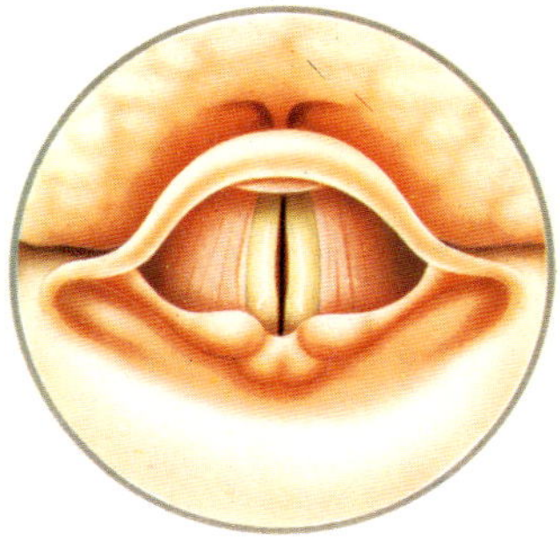

At the top of the windpipe is an area called the *larynx,* or voice box. Two bands of elastic cartilage are stretched across the larynx, with a small slit between them. These bands are the vocal cords and they can be stretched and relaxed by muscles. Air from the lungs passing through the slit makes the cords vibrate and this produces sound. The diagram above shows the cords stretched to produce a higher sound, and below they are relaxed to produce a deeper sound.

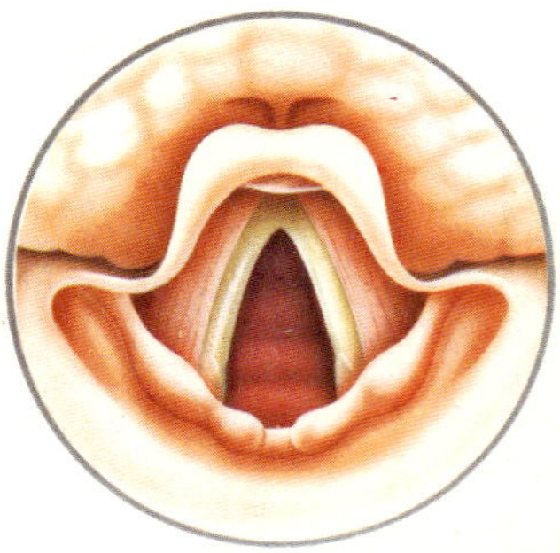

How We Speak

Like all sounds, speech is produced by vibrations. When speaking normally a steady airflow from the lungs passes around two membranes called the vocal cords, making them vibrate. These are located near the top of the throat. We control the pitch of the sound by altering the tension in the vocal cords—just as we can alter the pitch of a guitar by tightening or slackening the strings. The basic sound produced by the vocal cords is modified as it passes through the vocal tract. This consists of the upper throat and the mouth and nose cavities. By altering the shape of these passages, we affect the quality of sound produced.

The sounds we make using the vocal cords are described as *voiced*. But we do not always use the vocal cords when we speak. Whispered words, for example, are formed mainly by using the tongue and lips to modify a steady flow of air through the mouth. If you place one hand on your throat, you will feel the cords vibrate when you speak normally, but not when you whisper. Such sounds, made without using the vocal cords, are said to be *unvoiced*. Some sounds in normal speech are unvoiced too. These are the *unvoiced consonants*, such as *f* and *s*.

As the formation of speech sounds is such a complicated process, it is surprising how few people suffer from speech defects. Our speech mechanism involves the accurate control of numerous muscles, and a fault in only one part of the system can produce imperfect speech. However, most of us suffer temporary problems of this nature from time to time. For example, when we have a cold and get a blocked nose, our speech quality changes noticeably.

Noise

Noise is a general term for sounds we do not want to hear. A noise may disturb us when we are trying to relax. Or it may distract our attention when we are trying to concentrate on something else. In extreme cases, the noise may completely obscure a sound we want to hear.

The voiceprint on the left is an electronic graph of a person saying "Where are you?". It took one second to record.

Crackles caused by scratches on a gramophone record are a particularly irritating form of noise to someone trying to enjoy his favourite tune. But another person may regard the music itself as noise if it is not to his liking, especially if it is played loudly. In the same way, motor-cycle racing enthusiasts enjoy the atmosphere of excitement created by the roar of powerful engines at the track. But people living nearby merely complain about the noise. Just as beauty is said to be in the eye of the beholder, so some kinds of noise are in the ear of the listener.

Although noise often disturbs us, things could be so much worse. In fact, we are subjected to more noise than we realise, but our brain does a remarkable job in blocking out much of this unwanted sound. Unless we make a conscious effort to listen for noise, we are often totally unaware of its existence. The middle of a large city park is extremely quiet compared with the busy streets around it. But, if you listen, there is a noticeable background of traffic rumble, car horns, birdsong and other noises. Even the much louder noise of aircraft passing every few minutes can go unnoticed, unless it is so loud that it interferes with normal conversation. But, although our brain is very efficient at blocking out everyday sounds that we do not need to hear, it takes time to adapt to new sounds. People living near railway lines get used to the sound of trains and rarely find that their sleep is disturbed. But visitors staying with them for only a short time do not have time to adapt and are likely to suffer sleepless nights.

Noise plays an important part in sports such as drag racing. Fans enjoy the atmosphere created by the roar of powerful engines. But, sensibly, officals wear ear muffs to reduce the danger to their hearing.

Avoiding Noise

It has long been realised that extremely loud noises can cause deafness. But, in recent years, scientists have found that moderately loud sounds can do serious damage to our hearing too. And some low-pitched sounds can cause sickness, even when at a fairly low level. Because of these problems, the noise around us has come to be recognized as a form of air pollution.

Traffic noise gets worse every year as more and more vehicles take to the roads. In particular, there has been a great increase in the number of heavy, commercial vehicles, and these make more noise than most. Fortunately, their air-filled rubber tyres, designed to give a smooth ride, also help to reduce noise. Normally, the solid, steel-rimmed wheels of a small horse-drawn cart would make much more noise on the road than the huge tyres of a giant container truck. Rubber tyres are noisier only when abused by skidding or rapid breaking or acceleration. The intense screeching this can cause is often a problem for people living near a bend on a fast road. But the main problem with road vehicles is engine noise. This is reduced considerably by a silencer in the engine's exhaust system. Gases from the engine go through the silencer, where most of the explosive sounds they contain are absorbed.

Besides the roar of road traffic, the city dweller is subjected to noise from the powerful engines of jet aircraft. As on the roads, noise in the air is increasing all the time. Although we can learn to live with a fairly high noise level, people living near large airports may find the nose intolerable.

In most homes, single-pane windows are sufficient to reduce the noise from outside to a tolerable level. But, in extremely noisy locations, double glazing may be necessary. Most double glazing units are designed for good heat insulation properties, and have a fairly small gap between the two sheets of glass. Unfortunately, a much larger gap is required for good sound insulation. However, although not ideal for sound insulation purposes, standard double glazing is a considerable improvement on single-pane windows.

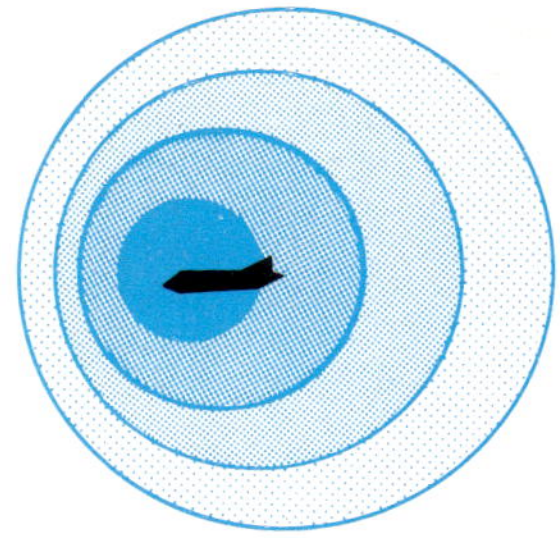

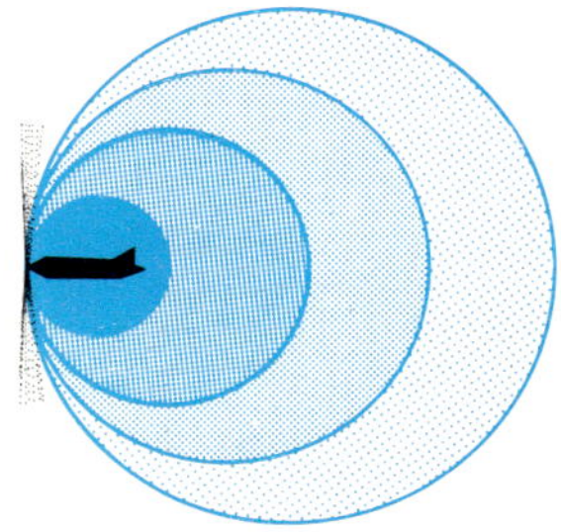

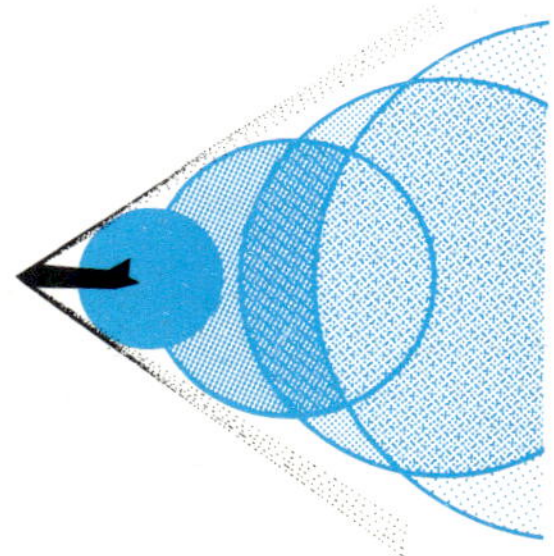

Sonic Booms

Another, quite different noise problem is caused by fast-flying jet aircraft. By moving through the air, an object causes an increase in air

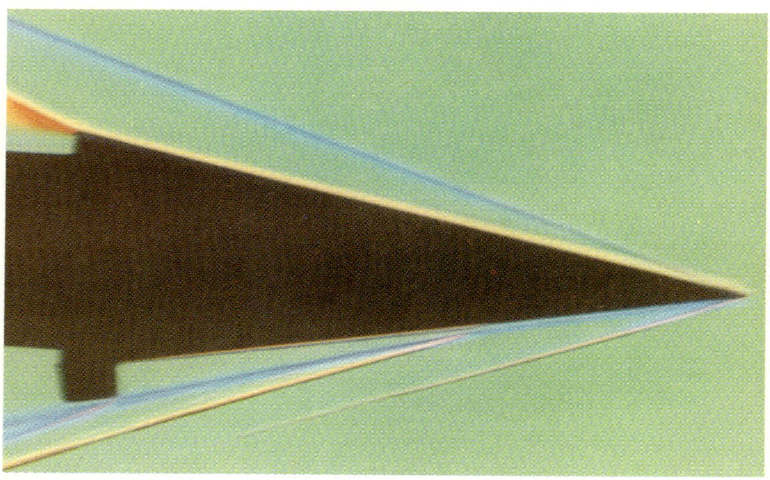

The picture on the left was taken in a wind tunnel by the schlieren process. The colours in this process show air shock waves building up to a sonic boom.

Left: Below the speed of sound an aircraft flies inside a pattern of pressure waves caused by its motion through the air. But the waves travelling at the speed of sound stay well ahead of the plane.

As the speed of sound is reached, the aircraft catches up with the pressure waves. They build up to form a shock wave at right angles to the direction of flight.

Above the speed of sound, the aircraft leaves the pressure waves behind, and the shock wave, still rooted to the plane, bends back. Sonic booms are heard on the ground as the shock wave passes.

pressure on its front surface. This high-pressure zone moves outwards through the air at the speed of sound, about 1,200 kilometres per hour (740 mph), and usually goes unnoticed. But some jet aircraft can travel at supersonic speeds—that is, above the speed of sound. When this occurs, the high pressure zone at the front is no longer moving fast enough to escape from the aircraft. As a result, the pressure builds up to form a shock wave. This moves along with the aircraft and spreads out to form a cone of intense high pressure. A loud bang, or sonic boom, is heard on the ground as the shock wave passes by. At the back of the aircraft, the opposite effect occurs, giving rise to a zone of greatly reduced pressure following close behind the high-pressure zone. On the ground, the effect is the same, and a second boom is heard. This accounts for the typical double bang caused by aircraft flying at supersonic speeds.

Sonic booms are quite unlike most other explosive noises. They are much lower in frequency and can be most alarming. In extreme cases, their high energy content can break windows and cause other minor damage to property.

Noise and Health

The ever-increasing noise from machines and tools has been a problem since the days of the Industrial Revolution. But, for a long time, people simply accepted that they might have to work in noisy surroundings. Little thought was given to the possibility that noise could be harmful. Scientific studies in this field did not begin until around 1940, by which time the situation was serious. In some industries, exposure to high noise levels was found to have damaged most workers' ears.

Strangely, rock musicians, who depend so much on their ears, do little to protect them. They usually ignore medical advice that the high sound levels they generate will cause their hearing to deteriorate. Worse still, their audiences suffer too, especially anyone near the stage. There is no doubt that, for enthusiasts, rock music is much more stimulating when played loudly. But, on some occasions, the level is so high that it makes the ears hurt. When this happens, the sound level has passed what is called the *threshold of feeling*. Our main sensation is then one of pain, rather than sound.

Rock music is more stimulating the more it is amplified. But the ear is a sensitive organ, and if it is subjected to prolonged intense sound it can be damaged.

The Nature of Sound

Compared with light, sound travels very slowly. This often becomes apparent at outdoor events, such as athletics meetings. When the gun is fired to start a race, spectators some distance away first see the smoke, and then hear the bang. In air, sound travels at about 330 metres (1100 feet) per second. Light, on the other hand, travels about a million times faster. This means that spectators 165 metres from the starter will see the smoke from his gun about half a second before they hear the bang.

Much longer time delays become apparent during thunderstorms. The lightning and thunder occur at the same instant. But we see the lightning first because the sound takes longer to reach us. The effect can be observed from a distance of several kilometres, so the time delay between the lightning and thunder can be quite long. Using a stopwatch, you can time the delay and work out how far away the storm is. Each three-second delay corresponds to a distance of about one kilometre. Or, if you prefer to work in imperial units, a delay of five seconds corresponds to a distance of about one mile. If you can see which direction the lightning is coming from, then, knowing the distance, you will be able to work out exactly where the storm is. And you can repeat the experiment at intervals to find out how the storm is moving. If the time delay gets shorter, then the storm is approaching. If the delay gets longer, then the storm is moving away from your area.

Sound is rarely used for measuring distances on land. But the technique is extremely useful underwater. A ship's echo sounder transmits bursts of sound waves from the hull. Echoes are reflected from the sea bed. From the time delay between the original signals and the reflections, the depth of water can be found. In a ship's sonar system, sound reflections are used to produce images on the screen of a cathode-ray tube. This can show a "sound map" of the area around the ship. From the display, called a PPI (Plan Position Indicator), the range (distance) and bearing (direction) of ships and other sound reflecting bodies can be seen. Fishing vessels can use this technique to locate shoals of fish.

Some sonar systems work at ultrasonic frequencies—that is, above the frequency range detectable by the human ear. Ultrasonic vibrations have many uses. Flaws inside metal objects can be detected using ultrasonics. For the flaws produce reflections that can be displayed on a screen. Doctors use ultrasonics to observe babies while they are still in their mother's womb. Producing a picture by means of ultrasonic reflections is much safer for the mother and child than using X-rays.

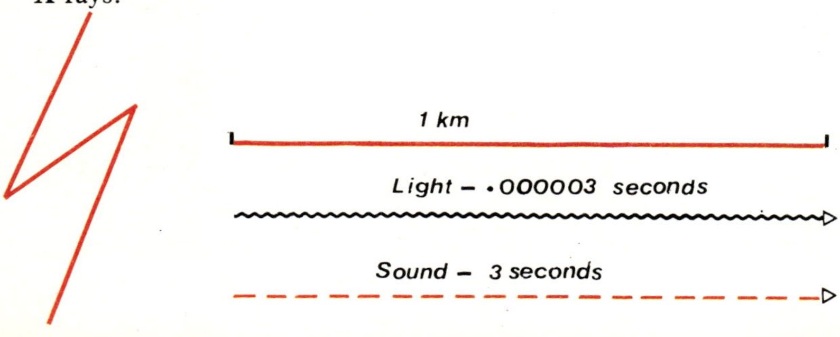

Nothing travels faster than light. At 300,000 kilometres per second, we see a lightning flash as it occurs. But sound is a comparative laggard. It takes air waves 3 seconds to cover one kilometre (1100 yards).

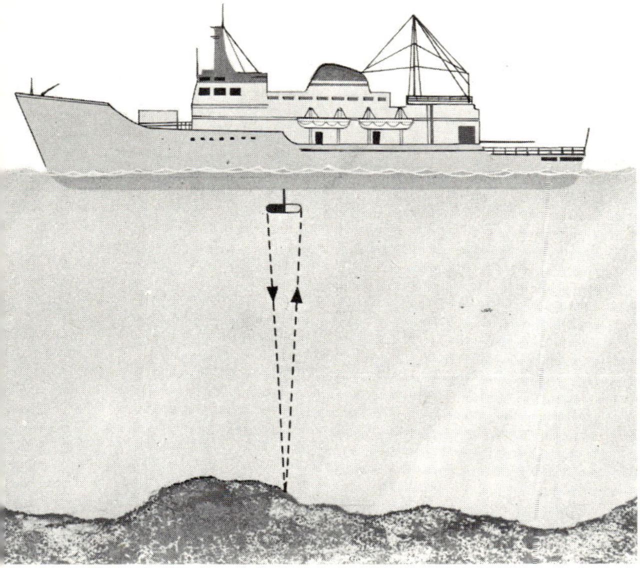

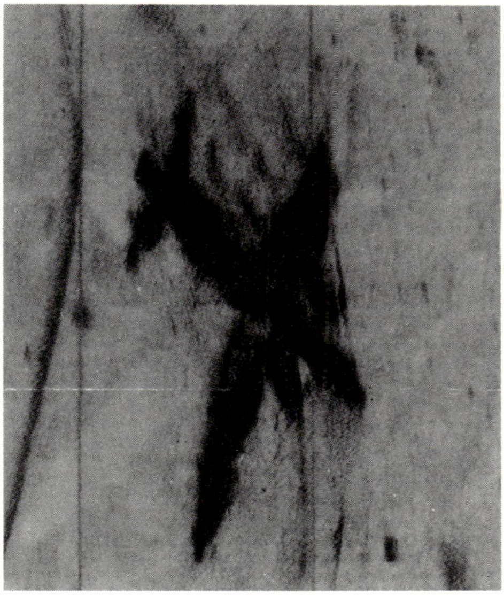

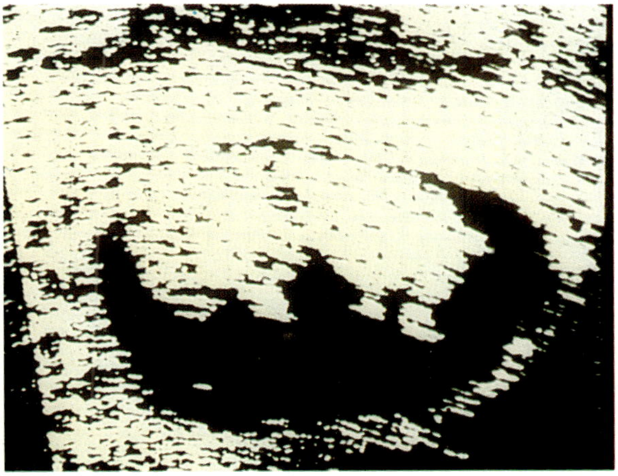

Above left: A survey ship uses sonar to map the sea bottom. The time taken for sound pulses to reach the bottom and be reflected back to the ship gives an accurate measure of the depth. On the right is a sonar picture of a World War II Wellington bomber discovered on the bottom of Loch Ness in Scotland.

Below: Ultrasonic vibrations are now used extensively to examine unborn babies. An ultrasonic image can be made easily, without the danger that using X-rays might cause. The ultrasonic picture on the left clearly shows the baby in the mother's womb.

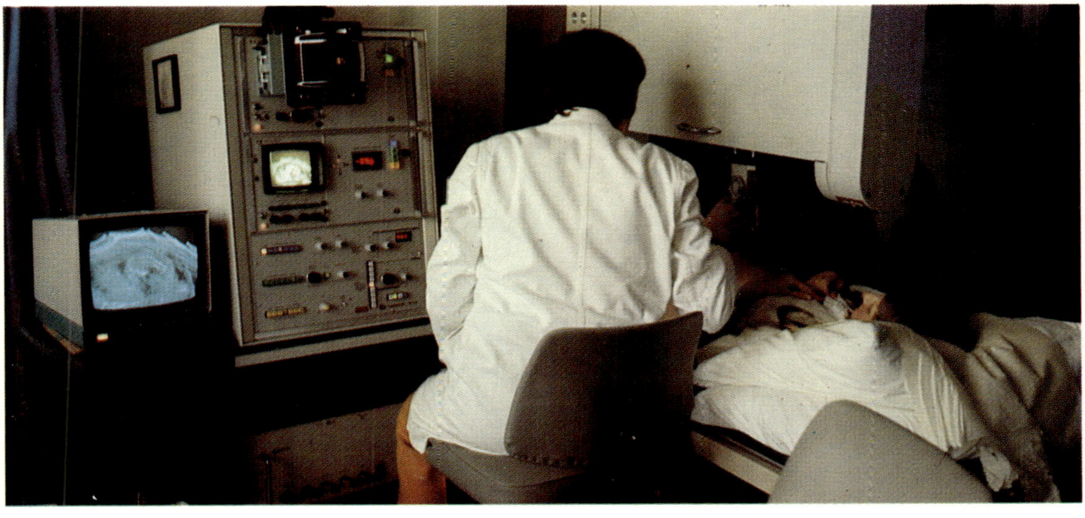

The Decibel
The decibel (dB) is one-tenth of a Bel, a unit for comparing two power or sound intensity levels. The Bel is a large unit, so decibels are used for most purposes. The decibel represents about the smallest change in sound intensity level that the human ear can detect. As it is a unit of comparison, an intensity given in decibels means nothing unless we know what the level is being compared with. So a level should be given as being so many decibels above or below some reference, or 'zero' level. We often compare the level of a sound with the intensity at which it would only just be audible. We would then say that the sound was so many decibels above the threshold of hearing. About 120 decibels above this level, the sensation of hearing starts to change to one of pain.

Except for the fact that they are higher in frequency, ultrasonic waves are identical to ordinary sound waves. In fact, what we call ultrasonic waves *are* sound waves to many animals. Dogs, for example, can hear high-frequency vibrations that are inaudible to the human ear. The response of the ear can vary considerably from one person to another. Older people cannot usually hear such high frequencies as younger people. So some high-frequency vibrations, clearly audible to the young, are ultrasonic as far as older people are concerned.

Vibrations and Waves

Sound is a series of vibrations picked up by the ears and interpreted as a sensation by the brain. In order to understand the behaviour of sound, we must first appreciate the nature of sound vibrations.

If we pluck a guitar string, we can see the blur it makes as it vibrates rapidly to and fro. This movement disturbs the surrounding air, causing it to vibrate too. The vibrations travel through the air to our ears, and force our eardrums to vibrate. Inside each ear, the vibrations are converted into electrical signals that our brain interprets as sound.

Sound needs a medium—some solid, liquid or gas—through which to travel. In outer space, you would not hear even a cannon fired a few inches away, for there would be no medium to transfer the vibrations of the explosion to your ears. You would be able to see the cannon because light travels in an entirely different way to sound. Like radio signals, light is a form of electromagnetic radiation, and this can travel through empty space. However, despite this basic difference, sound and light have one important feature in common. Both travel from their source as disturbances called *waves*. But it would be misleading to think of sound travelling along wavy lines. For, under normal conditions, sound travels from one point to another in a straight line. And the vibrations by which the sound is transmitted take place along the line of travel. What happens is that the to-and-fro movements of the vibrating body emitting the sound alternately increase and decrease the pressure of the surrounding air. The compressions and rarefactions thus formed travel through the air. It is important to understand that the air itself does not travel from the source to the listener. It is only the disturbances that are transmitted. In a similar way, if you fix one end of a rope to a wall, you can send a ripple along the rope by quickly flicking the other end. The ripple moves along the rope because the disturbance you make by moving the end is passed on from one part of the rope to the next. In the case of the rope, the disturbance is at right-angles to the direction in which it travels. With sound, as previously explained, the disturbances are along the direction of travel.

Anything that vibrates within a certain range of frequencies causes air waves that we hear as sound. The horsehair of a violin bow is rough enough to make the violin strings vibrate as it is drawn over them. The four strings give the player four basic notes. To obtain other notes, the player shortens the vibrating strings by pressing them down on the fingerboard – the shorter the string, the higher the frequency of vibration and the higher the note.

To understand how sound is transmitted through the air, it is best to consider what happens to a single, horizontal line of air molecules, the tiny particles of gas and water vapour that make up our atmosphere. Air has mass, so we can regard the molecules as tiny weights suspended in space. Another property important in sound transmission is the *elasticity* of the medium. This is concerned with the ability of a substance to return to its original shape and size when some force acting on it is removed. In everyday life, we usually associate elasticity with rubber or other obviously springy substances. But all substances have some degree of elasticity. You can demonstrate that air has elastic properties by blocking the end of a bicycle pump and

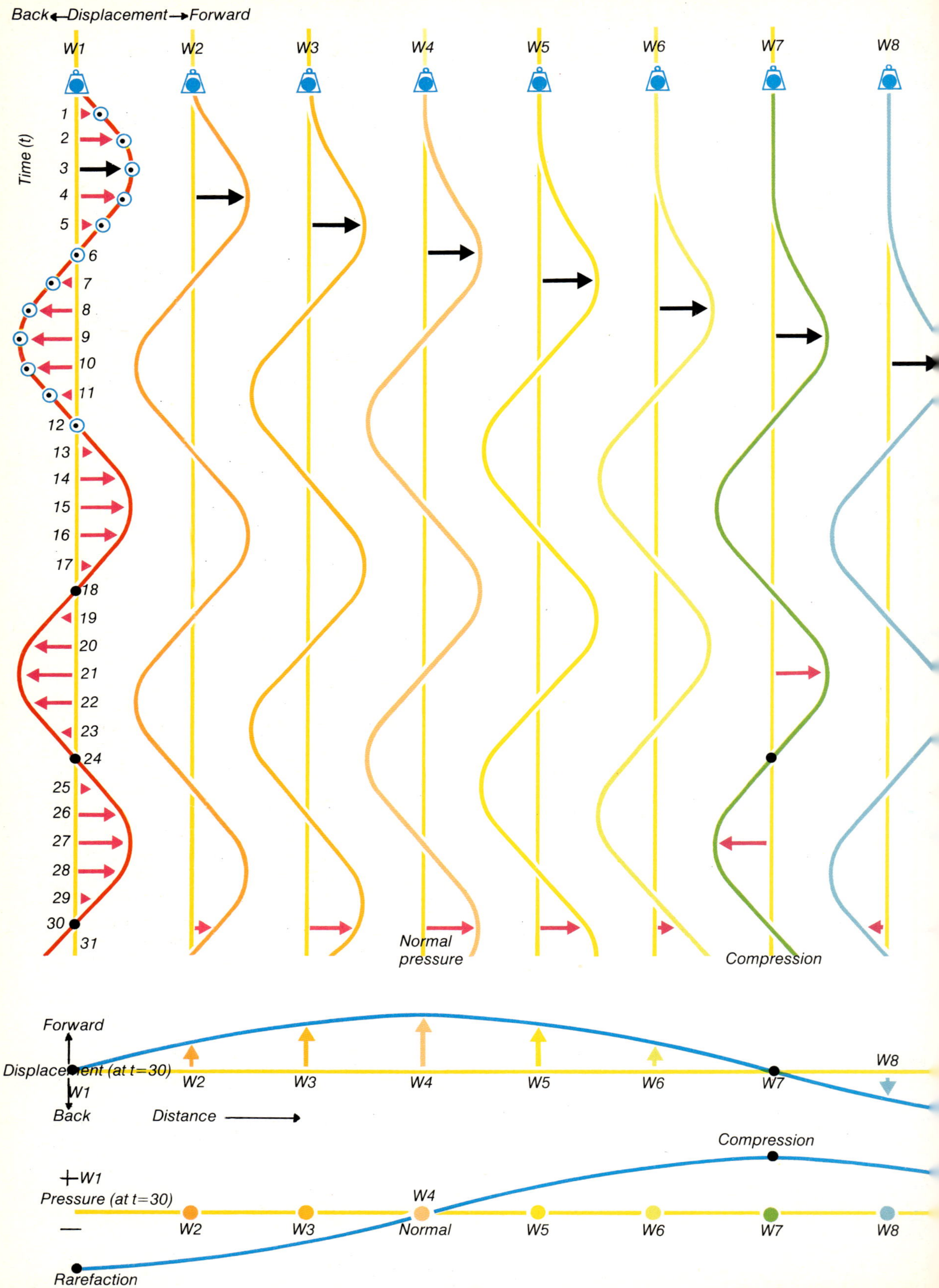

Back ← Displacement → Forward
W1
W2
W3
W4
W5
W6
W7
W8
Time (t)
1
2
3
4
5
6
7
8
9
10
11
12
13
14
15
16
17
18
19
20
21
22
23
24
25
26
27
28
29
30
31
Normal pressure
Compression
Forward
Displacement (at t=30)
Back
Distance
+W1
Pressure (at t=30)
—
Normal
Rarefaction

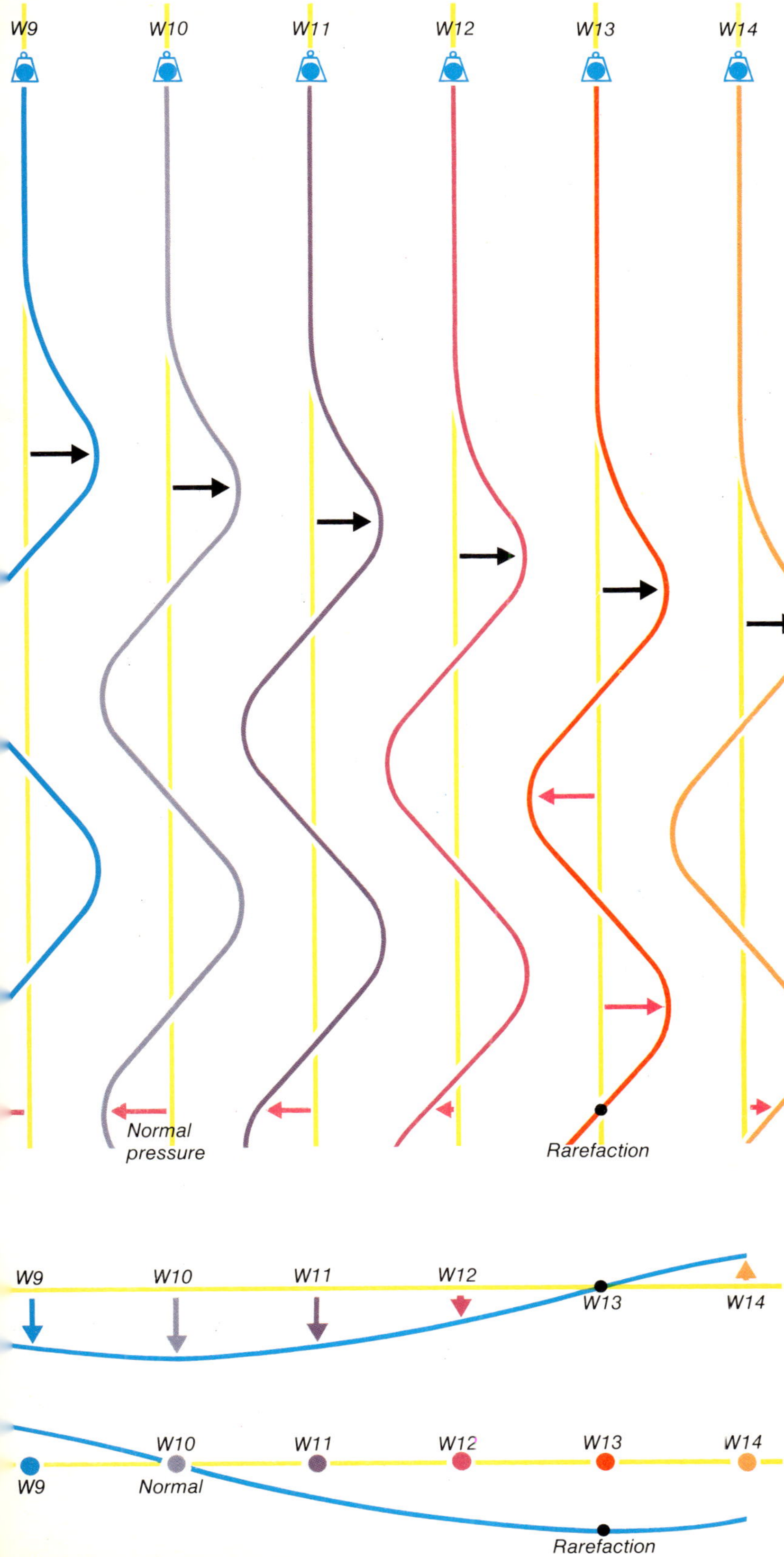

One way of showing how sound moves through the air is to consider what happens to a row of air molecules. Think of the molecules as tiny weights joined by springs (A). If we move the left-hand weight to and fro, the vibrations will spread along the line, every weight vibrating at the same frequency. But, as the weights start vibrating at slightly different times, each one will be out of step with its neighbours. W1 reaches maximum displacement to the right at time t=3 on the time scale. W2 does not reach this stage until t=4. Weight W7 does not reach maximum displacement to the right until t=9. By this time W1 has reached maximum displacement to the left. W7 is exactly one half-cycle behind W1 – the two movements are in opposite phase. W13 is one complete cycle behind W1 – these two weights are in phase. Graph B shows the displacement of the particles of air at a particular instant – in this case at time t=30. The vertical scale shows the displacement of each particle at this instant. The horizontal scale shows the distance of each particle from the first one. From this graph and graph A it can be seen that at t=30, W7 is under maximum compression – W6 and W8 are being forced towards it. W13 is at a point of least pressure – W12 and W14 are going away from it. It can therefore be seen that maximum and minimum pressure points occur when particle displacement is zero. Graph C shows how air pressure varies over a distance for the same particles as in graphs A and B. See pages 20 to 21 for a fuller explanation of these graphs.

then pushing in the handle. Assuming that there are no leaks, the air will spring back to its original volume and push the handle out when you let it go. So, if we represent our sound path through the air by a row of suspended weights, we must connect the weights with springs to simulate the elasticity of the medium. Now we can investigate what happens when a vibrating object is allowed to act on our model.

If we move the left-hand weight to and fro, we will find that the vibrations soon spread along the line. The speed at which they spread will depend on the types of springs and weights used. With weak springs and heavy weights, the vibrations will travel along the line relatively slowly. On the other hand, with stiffer springs and lighter weights, the speed of transmission will be much higher. In practice, this means that the velocity (speed in a given direction) of sound is determined by the properties of the medium through which it travels. And, as these properties change with temperature, so the speed of sound will change too. At a temperature of 0°C sound travels through the air at about 330 metres (1100 feet) per second. In pure water at the same temperature, the velocity of sound is about 1410 metres (4600 feet) per second. This rises with temperature to around 1560 metres (5100 feet) per second at 80°C.

If, on our model, we vibrate the first weight at a steady rate, or *frequency*, soon the whole line of weights will be vibrating. And all will vibrate at exactly the same frequency as the first one. But, as they start vibrating at slightly different times, each one will be a little out of step with its neighbours. The movements of the weights are, therefore, said to be *out of phase* with one another.

In order to investigate these movements in more detail, it is convenient to show how each weight moves over a period of time. This has been done in the diagram on the previous pages by drawing a graph below each weight. These graphs are formed by first marking, at regular time intervals, the displacement of each weight from its original position. Smooth curves are then drawn through the plotted positions. This construction has been shown in detail for the graph under the left-hand weight (W1).

As you can see, all the weights are equally spaced and stationary at the start (0 on the time scale). Then, as W1 is moved to the right, the next one W2, starts to move too. It is soon moving in the same manner as W1, but always reaching any particular stage in the cycle of vibration just after W1. For example, W1 reaches a maximum, or peak of displacement to the right at time $t = 3$ on the time scale. But W2 does not reach this stage until time $t = 4$. Farther along the line, the delay is much longer. By time $t = 3$, weight W7 has hardly moved. And it does not reach maximum displacement to the right until $t = 9$. By this time, W1 has already reached maximum displacement to the left. Although W7 still copies the movements of W1, it is exactly one half-cycle behind. In cases like this, the two movements are said to be of *opposite phase*. Still farther along the line, W13 is one complete cycle behind W1. These two weights therefore move exactly in step with each other, and are said to be *in phase*. And W14 is in phase with W2.

The graphs we have discussed show how the weights move over a period of time. And similar graphs can be used to represent sound waves in air by showing how the air particles move. For convenience, we usually draw these graphs from left to right across the page. Time is shown along the horizontal axis, and particle displacement on the vertical axis. For most purposes, one such graph is sufficient, as the air

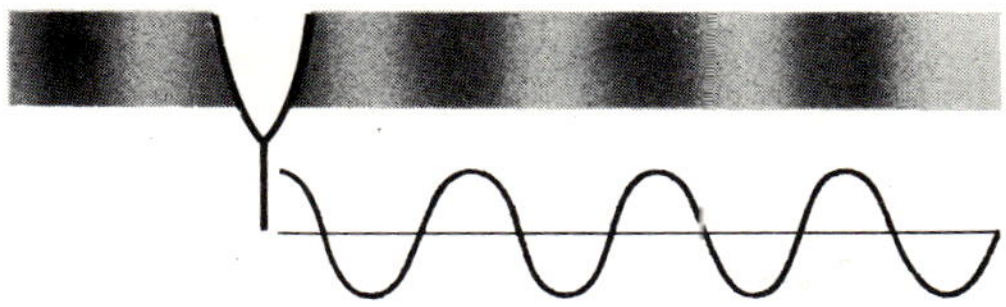

Sound waves are alternate compressions and rarefactions of air. They are formed when a tuning fork vibrates. As the prongs of the fork move outwards, a compression is formed

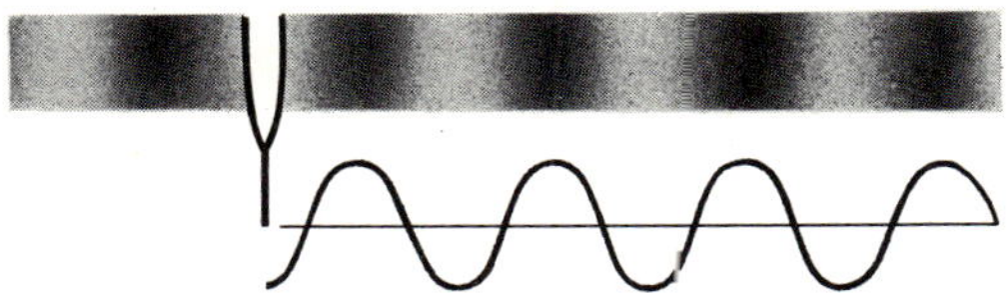

As the prongs of the tuning fork move inwards, a rarefaction forms.

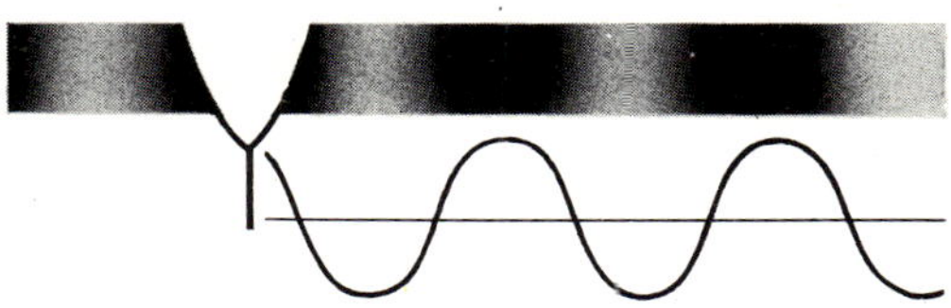

If the fork is struck harder, the compressions are greater, and the sound is louder.

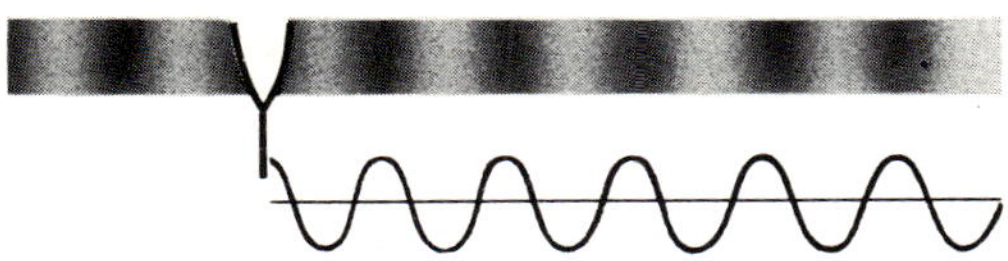

If a smaller fork is struck, the vibration (frequency) is more rapid and the wavelength is shorter. A higher-pitched sound is heard.

particles in all locations eventually move in a similar fashion. However, at any instant, the individual displacements are different. But, instead of drawing a series of graphs, there is a much simpler way of showing this. For we can draw a single graph to show the displacement of various particles at one particular instant. In our diagram showing the weights, the graph along the bottom does precisely this for the weights at time t = 30. For each weight, the displacement has been plotted on the vertical axis. The horizontal scale shows the distance of each weight from the first one. The basic shape of this graph is the same as that of the others (ignoring their initial stages).

Earlier, we talked of sound being transmitted through the air as a series of compressions and rarefactions. At any instant, you can find out where these zones are by looking at the particle positions on the diagram. For a point under maximum compression has particles being forced towards it from both sides. If we look at the situation when t = 30, we can see that W7 is under maximum compression, and W6 and W8 are both displaced towards it. Similarly, W13 is at a point of maximum rarefaction, or minimum pressure. In this case, the particles either side are displaced away from it. As you can see from the diagram, the maximum and minimum pressure points occur where the particle displacement is zero. Either side of W4 and W10, the pressures are equal. So, at these points, the air pressure is the same as it was before the sound waves were generated. Note that such points occur where the displacement is a maximum in either direction. In later chapters, we shall see the importance of these relationships, especially when considering the design of musical wind instruments, and sound absorbers for studios and concert halls.

For some purposes, it is convenient to represent sound waves as a graph showing how the air pressure varies over a distance, or how the pressure at a given point varies over a period of time. In each case, the shape of the graph obtained resembles that of the graph showing the particle vibrations. Having so many ways to represent sound waves may make the subject seem complicated. But we usually choose just one type of graph showing the particular quantities we want to study. For example, if we are interested in the length of a sound wave, we must use a graph with distance (not time) along the horizontal axis.

Frequency and Wavelength

The rate, or *frequency*, of a vibration is the number of complete to-and-fro movements, or *cycles*, that occur in each second. Sound vibrations are in the range extending from about 20 to 20,000 cycles per second. In the International System of Units (S.I.), the name hertz (Hz) has been given to a unit of one cycle per second. So we say that the sound frequency range is about 20 to 20,000 hertz. This can also be written as 20Hz to 20kHz, the small k standing for kilo, meaning thousand. Sounds we describe as deep, or low, are caused by low frequency vibrations. Shrill, or high-pitched sounds are produced by bodies vibrating at relatively high frequencies.

Wavelength means the physical length of one complete wave. This is determined by the frequency of vibration and the velocity (speed in a given direction) at which the waves travel. Consider just one vibration. If this occurs slowly, then the distance that the wave spreads during the time of the vibration will be relatively long. Also, if the vibrations travel extremely quickly, then each wave will be spread over a long distance. Usually, however, we can assume that the velocity of the waves is constant. So the only factor that can alter the

The pipe organ is the largest and most powerful of all musical instruments. It can have as many as 40,000 pipes, measuring from a few centimetres to over 19 metres (60 feet) in length – the larger the pipe, the deeper the note. When air is forced into the largest pipes its vibration creates a rumbling musical note that can be felt throughout the entire building. This organ is in Salisbury Cathedral, England.

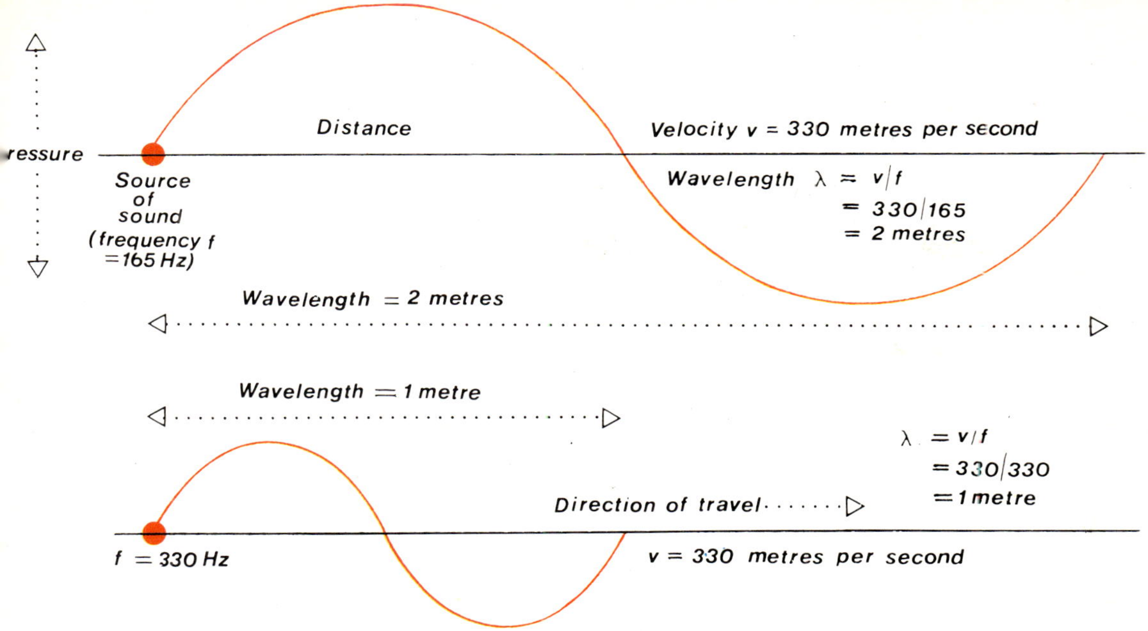

wavelength is the frequency of the vibrations. Low frequency vibrations will give relatively long waves. And high frequency vibrations will give shorter waves.

Suppose that we want to find the wavelength of a sound that has a frequency of 165 hertz. As there are 165 complete vibrations every second, one vibration will occur in every 1/165 second. Now sound travels through air at about 330 metres per second. So, in 1/165 second, it travels 330 × 1/165 metres = 2 metres. This means that, by the time one complete vibration has been emitted by the source of sound, the front of the wave will be 2 metres away. So the whole wave occupies a distance of 2 metres, and this is, therefore, the wavelength of the vibration.

In general, wavelength is given by the formula:

$$\lambda = v/f$$

where λ (the Greek letter lambda) is wavelength in metres,
v is the velocity of the waves in metres per second,
and f is the frequency of the vibrations in hertz (cycles per second).

This formula enables us to work out the wavelength of any sound if we know its frequency and velocity. Taking the velocity of sound in air as 330 metres per second, we can now work out the range of wavelengths of sound waves. At the bottom end of the frequency range, a frequency of 20Hz has a wavelength of 330/20 = 16.5 metres. At the top end of the range, a frequency of 20kHz gives a wavelength of 330/20,000 = 0.0165 metres, or 16.5 millimetres.

This relationship between wavelength and frequency is particularly important in the design of musical wind instruments. For the length of such an instrument determines the longest wavelength that it can produce. For example, a piccolo, being quite small, produces relatively short sound waves, which therefore have a high frequency and pitch. At the other end of the scale, long organ pipes produce the lowest notes of all wind instruments.

The number of complete air vibrations per second (the number of Hertz) decide whether a sound is low or high-pitched. Human adults can hear from about 20 Hz to 20,000 Hz, but the ear's sensitivity to high-frequency sounds decreases as a person gets older. Children can usually hear sounds higher than 20,000 Hz, and dogs higher still.

Acoustics

Right: The Greek amphitheatre at Epidaurus. These ancient amphi-theatres were so skilfully designed acoustically that every word spoken by an actor in the centre of the stage could be heard clearly by all the audience – in this case a possible 14,000 people.

Acoustics is the science of sound. But the word is often used as a vague term to describe how a room or hall affects sounds made in it. If someone is giving a lecture, and the voice sounds so boomy that it is difficult to understand, the room would be described as having "bad acoustics". However, music played in the same room might sound quite acceptable. The room would then be described as having "good acoustics". Clearly then, the acoustic properties required of a room depend on how that room is to be used. The task of the acoustic engineer is to ensure that these requirements are achieved. To understand how this is done, we must consider what gives a room its own particular acoustic qualities.

Sound Reflections

Hard surfaces are good reflectors of sound. If we shout a "hello" towards a distant cliff face, the reflected sound waves give rise to a distant echo. If the cliff is a long way away, the time delay between the shout and its echo could be several seconds. Inside a room, the situation is quite different. Reflections occur at the floor, walls and ceiling, so the sound bounces around the room, forming a complex pattern. Instead of producing a distinct echo, the numerous reflections combine to give a continuous effect known as *reverberation*. This extends the duration of the sound, causing it to die away gradually instead of ending abruptly. The effect is particularly noticeable in bathrooms, where the hard surfaces ensure good reflection of sound. Such a room is said to be relatively "live" or "echoey". In a living room, with heavy curtains, a thick carpet and soft furnishings, sounds die away much more quickly. When sound strikes a soft surface, most of its energy is absorbed, instead of being reflected. Acoustically, such a room is described as being relatively "dead" or "dry".

People who sing to themselves at home tend to do this mostly in the bathroom. The sound waves reflected from the hard surfaces in the room combine to give a higher sound level, or *intensity*. This is why the voice sounds more powerful than in other surroundings. And the reverberation helps to give a "smoother" quality to the voice, blending the sounds together and filling the gaps between them. In addition, the reverberation actually helps us to sing better.

When we talk or sing, our ears pick up the sound we make and send signals to the brain. If there is anything wrong with the sound, the brain automatically changes the signals it sends to the muscles controlling the voice. As a result, the sound is modified, and comes closer in quality and volume to the sound we wish to make. You can demonstrate how this *feedback* of signals to the brain helps a person to control his voice. Just get someone to talk to you while listening to loud music on headphones. The person will speak much louder than normal. This is because no feedback from his voice is reaching his

ears. The brain interprets this as "not enough volume", and makes him raise his voice. On taking off the headphones, he will immediately lower his voice to its normal volume.

As reverberation prolongs the duration of the sounds we make, it gives the brain a better chance of assessing the quality and applying any necessary corrections. So we end up making a better sound than we would if there were no reverberation.

How Much Reverberation?

Although a certain amount of reverberation enhances the singing voice, too much can spoil it. In extreme cases, the words overlap so much that it is difficult to understand any of them. For the same

Exact sound measurements are best taken when there are no disturbing sound reflections. The engine noise of this truck is being tested in an *anechoic chamber,* a room designed to be without echo.

reason, excessive reverberation must be avoided in rooms where lectures or speeches are to be given. But this does not mean that reverberation should be eliminated in such a room. For talking in an acoustically dead room is most unpleasant for the speaker. Without the feedback provided by reverberation, he feels that his voice cannot be reaching the audience. And trying to speak more loudly seems to have little effect. A small amount of reverberation is, therefore, necessary to reassure the speaker that all is well.

Obtaining the desired amount of reverberation in a room is one of the acoustic engineer's main tasks. This is accomplished by using various materials and devices to absorb just the right amount of sound. To measure reverberation, the engineer finds the time taken by a sound to decay to one millionth of its original intensity. This duration is called the *reverberation time* of the room. For sound broadcasting, drama and talks studios would typically have reverberation times of about 0.3 second. For orchestral performances, the reverberation time would range from about one second for the smallest studio to about two seconds for the largest.

When a column of air vibrates, it gives out a musical note; the longer the column, the lower the note. This can be demonstrated by blowing across the open end of a tube and moving a cork to increase or decrease the length of the column of air in the tube. The slide of a trombone similarly alters the length of the column of air that is allowed to vibrate, and thus alters the sound produced.

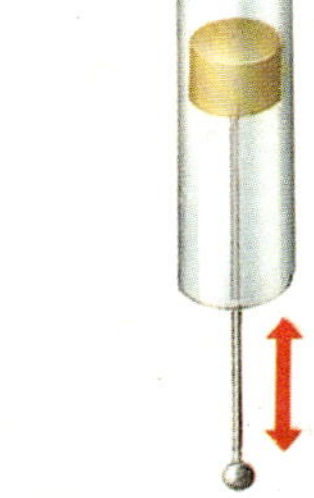

Room Resonances

Anything that can vibrate has a *natural resonant frequency*. This is the frequency at which it vibrates most easily. If you blow into an "empty" bottle, the air inside will tend to vibrate at its natural resonant frequency. This is why the bottle usually emits the same musical note when you blow into it. Similarly, when you pluck a guitar string, the note it emits corresponds to its natural resonant frequency. This can be altered by fingering the string to shorten its effective length. The shorter the length that can vibrate, the higher the frequency of sound.

In rooms with sound-reflecting surfaces, resonances can occur in the air. In a simple, rectangualar room, the air between a pair of opposite walls behaves rather like a guitar string. Its "ends" are fixed, while the rest is free to vibrate. (The air particles actually touching the wall cannot move away from it as they are held in contact by the surrounding air pressure.) At the natural resonant frequency of the

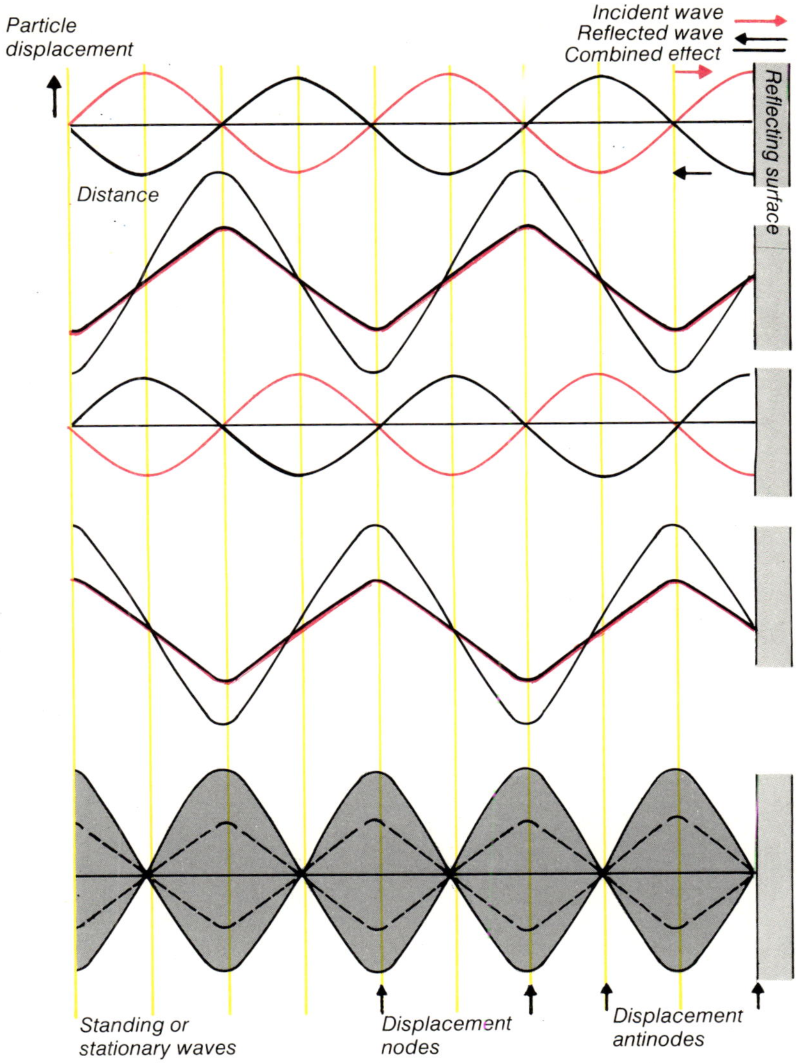

STANDING WAVES

At the reflecting surface, the resultant displacement is always zero. At the instant shown, it is also zero at all other points.

A quarter cycle later, the incident wave has moved right, and the reflected wave left. The displacement is now at a maximum.

Another quarter cycle later, the incident and reflected waves again cancel. So the resultant is again zero at all points.

After another quarter cycle, the two component waves again act together. The resultant displacement is, therefore, at a maximum.

The standing or stationary waves are shown by drawing the resultant displacement at various times. Zero and maximum displacement have been shown as solid lines. The broken lines show intermediate values. Points that experience no particle displacement are called displacement nodes. Points where maximum displacement occurs are called displacement antinodes. Note that the displacement nodes experience maximum *pressure* and are, therefore, pressure antinodes.

system, air particles mid-way between the walls will vibrate most of all. Away from the centre, the vibrations decrease, eventually reaching zero at the wall surfaces. This fixed sound wave pattern is called a *stationary wave pattern*. When we considered a sound wave moving through the air (page 20), all the air particles went through the same vibrations, one after the other. Here the situation is different because the waves are reflected back by the walls. The standing wave pattern is formed by the combination of waves travelling in opposite directions.

For a sound wave moving through the air, the distance between regions of zero particle displacement (nodes) is one-half wavelength (see page 22). The same is true of the nodes in a standing wave pattern. This enables us to find the resonant frequency. Suppose, for example, that the walls are 3 metres apart. As this is the distance between two nodes, it must equal one-half wavelength. So the wavelength (λ) must be 6 metres. Frequency is equal to velocity divided by wavelength, giving us 330/6 = 55 hertz.

As you can see from the diagram above, a whole series of standing wave patterns can occur between a pair of walls. As a result, resonances will be heard at various frequencies. Assuming that the three dimensions of the room are all different, there will then be three different series of resonant frequencies for the room. And these can interact to produce further resonances. This is why, if you try humming in a bathroom, you will find many notes that sound distinctly louder than the others. However, in large rooms, the resonant frequencies that occur in the audible range are so closely grouped that the ear cannot detect any changes in sound level throughout the entire musical range.

Acoustic Treatment

Acoustic treatment usually means the use of sound absorbent materials and devices to obtain the desired reverberation characteristics in a room. It is fairly easy to absorb sound, but the problem lies in ensuring that the absorption is correct at all frequencies throughout the audio range. Ideally, the reverberation time should be slightly longer at high and low frequencies compared with its value at mid-range frequencies. This compensates for the uneven response of the ear to fairly quiet sounds. So it *sounds* as if the reverberation is the same at all frequencies.

Porous furnishings, such as carpets and curtains are good sound absorbers. Air particles in these materials are set in motion by the sound waves. As the particles vibrate, they rub against the material.

A large hall has good acoustics if it reflects only useful sound to listeners. A balance has to be set between proper sound reflection of the human voice, single instruments and large orchestras. The acoustic engineer uses various materials and devices to absorb just the right amount of sound. In the hall on the left acoustic brickwork on either side of the stage helps to reflect and scatter the sound and ensure even dispersion. Overhead sound reflectors (below) are used to balance the sound in all parts of the hall.

Architects build model halls fitted with seats and blocks to simulate people. Sound readings and acoustic adjustments ensure near-perfect sound when the actual hall is built. This model hall is 6 metres (20 feet) long and 3.5 metres (11 feet) across.

This friction converts some of their sound energy into heat. At high frequencies, the particles move faster. So more heat is generated, and more sound energy lost.

Walls are often treated by applying a layer of absorbent material, such as fibreglass or rock wool and covering it with perforated panels. The surface of the panels reflects high frequencies, thus preventing excessive absorption in this range. Some radio drama studios have a variety of panels hinged to the walls. The studio acoustics can be changed quickly simply by exposing a different type of surface.

The membrane absorber consists of a panel of hardboard, or other non-porous material, covering an airtight cavity. The panel tends to resonate at one particular frequency, rather like a drumskin. When sound at this frequency strikes the panel, it vibrates to and fro, absorbing maximum energy from the waves. At other frequencies, it is less inclined to move and, therefore, reflects a higher proportion of sound. Membrane absorbers are used for absorption at low frequencies.

The Helmholtz resonator is usually a wall cavity with a narrow opening to the room. The device absorbs maximum sound energy at resonance, which is usually in the low to mid-frequency range.

Changing the furnishings in a studio can dramatically alter its acoustics. Adding several well-padded chairs could greatly increase the sound absorption in a small studio. On the other hand, adding a large conference table would produce extra reflections and give a more reverberant sound. In concert halls, the most variable factor is the audience. For each person acts as a sound absorber. And the amount of clothing worn determines how much sound a person absorbs. In winter, people wear heavier clothing, so they absorb more sound. As a result, concert halls sound deader in winter. Besides seasonal changes, there are also long term changes in fashion. In Victorian times, ladies tended to wear quite bulky clothes. So the mini-skirted ladies attending concerts in the 1960s were poor sound absorbers compared with their Victorian predecessors. This caused acoustic problems at London's Albert Hall, for the increased reverberation was spoiling the music. The situation was counteracted by suspending saucer-shaped sound absorbers at various places in the hall.

Sound in Focus

A particular problem occurs with circular buildings. The internal walls, being concave, tend to focus sound waves so that they concentrate at certain points. In a concert hall, this effect can make some instruments sound much too loud to some members of the audience. Sound focusing also occurs in the domed roofs of many buildings. When a person up in the gallery whispers, someone a few metres away may hear nothing. But the sound may be heard quite clearly at the other side of the gallery. This effect can be heard in the Capitol Building in Washington, D.C., and in the "whispering gallery" at St. Paul's Cathedral, London.

As concave surfaces focus sound waves, they should be avoided in rooms where sound quality is important. Ideally, randomly placed *convex* surfaces should be used to reflect and scatter the sound to ensure its even dispersion throughout the room.

Soundproofing

Soundproofing, or sound insulation, is concerned with preventing sound from entering or leaving a room, building, or other enclosure. Different types of buildings have different requirements as far as sound insulation is concerned. Broadcasting and recording studios obviously need special attention, although requirements here vary too. For example, a higher level of background noise can be tolerated in a talks studio than in one used for music. This is because, during a talk, the microphone is always quite close to the speaker. Therefore, the background noise picked up is relatively weak in comparison. But, in a music studio, a microphone may be covering a group of players some distance away. So, during quiet passages, any background noise may not sound much softer than the music itself. Another problem is that unwanted sounds are generally more annoying when listening to music than when listening to speech.

Noise can reach a studio through the air or through the structure of the building. Reduction of airborne noise entering the studio directly is fairly simple. The windows and doors are made airtight, and double or triple glazing is used. Most studios have heavy double doors as further protection from airborne noise. Once a room has been sealed in this way, an air-conditioning system becomes essential. This can itself introduce noise unless precautions are taken. So special baffles are placed in the air ducts to absorb any noise in the incoming air.

Structure-borne noise includes impacts from footsteps, hammering and similar sounds. These are eliminated by using resilient (springy) materials to link the studio structure with the main shell of the building.

Sounds of Music

When a vibrating body emits sound waves with a steady frequency, or rate, we hear a musical note. In musical instruments, the vibrating body is often a stretched string or skin, or a column of air. The *pitch* of the sound produced—how high or low it is in the musical range—is determined by the frequency of the vibrations. This can usually be varied in some way, so that the instrument can produce a range of notes. For example, shortening the effective length of a guitar string by pressing it against the fingerboard will make it vibrate faster, and thus produce a higher-pitched note. A similar effect occurs when one of the holes along a clarinet is uncovered, thus shortening the length of the vibrating air column in the instrument. Besides altering the physical length of the vibrating body, there are other ways of changing the frequency of vibration. In most wind instruments, for example, this can happen when the player changes the tension of his lips. In fact, on the bugle, this is the only means by which the player can control the pitch of the notes produced. And changing the tension of the strings of a guitar will alter the pitch of the notes produced. This is how guitars, violins and many other stringed instruments are tuned before a performance. The tensions are carefully adjusted while listening to the notes produced until their pitch sounds correct. Increasing the tension causes an increase in frequency and, therefore, pitch.

Scales

The musical note commonly used for checking the tuning of instruments has a frequency of 440 hertz. This note is called A. On a

BEATS

When any two notes sound together, one also hears the difference of their frequencies. This does not become apparent until the notes are close in frequency—that is, one is slightly out of tune with the other. Then their difference will be heard as a slow rise and fall in volume. This effect is known as beats. Listening for beats is a very good way of tuning an instrument.

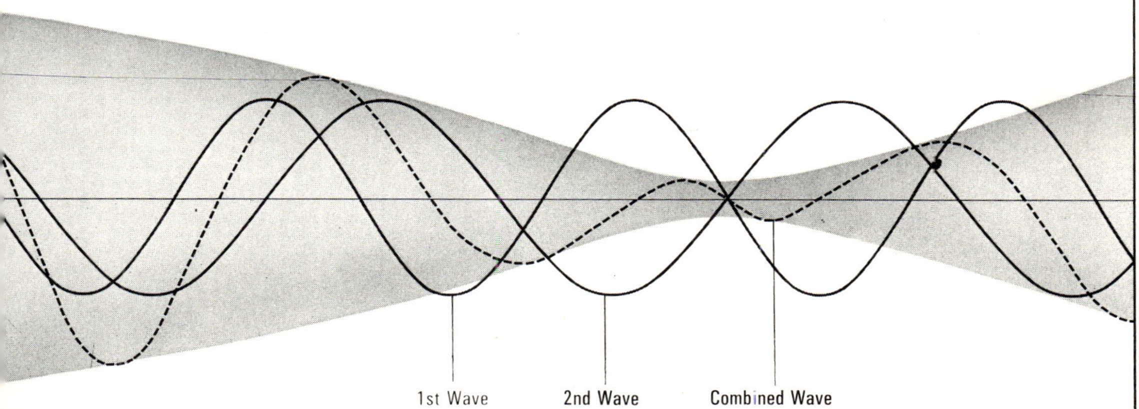

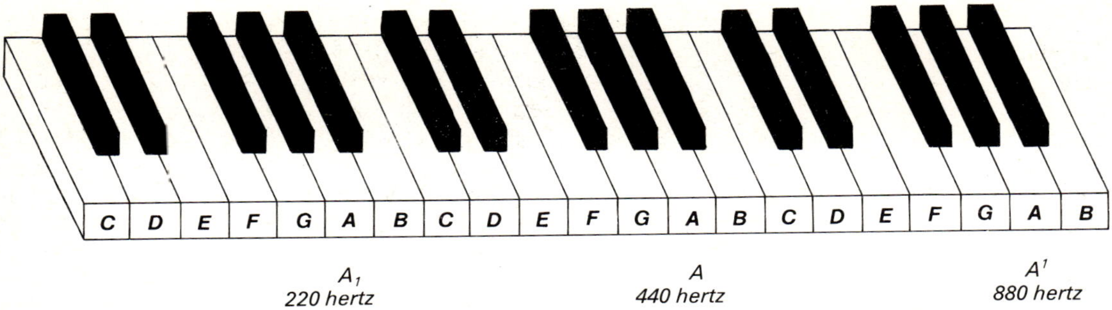

Part of a piano keyboard showing the frequencies of three As, each an octave apart.

piano keyboard, it is located a little to the right of the centre. Doubling the frequency of any note increases its pitch by the musical "distance", or *interval,* called an *octave.* A frequency of 880 hertz therefore corresponds to the next highest A note, which is written as A^1. And the note A_1, which is an octave below A, has a frequency of 220 hertz.

The word *octave* comes from the Latin for eight, as we divide this musical interval into a scale of eight notes (including both first and last). The scale of C major, for example, consists of the notes C, D, E, F, G, A, B and C, and so on through the other octaves. As you can see from the chart above, these are all white notes on the piano keyboard. In a system called the *tonic sol-fa,* the notes of such a scale are written as doh, ray, me, fah, sol, lah, te and doh. The note on which a scale begins (C in this case) is called the *keynote*, and is always called doh.

If you count the black notes as well as the white ones, you will see that it actually takes twelve steps on the piano to get from one C to the next. Each of these steps is called a *semitone.* In our scale, some steps are semitones, but most are equal to two semitones, or one *tone.* The seven steps in our scale, going from one doh to the next, are as follows: 2, 2, 1, 2, 2, 2 and 1 semitones. All major scales follow this pattern, with a step of only one semitone from me to fah, and from te to doh.

As we have seen, the arrangements of the piano keyboard is such that the scale of C major is played using only white notes. Where a step of two semitones is required, there is a black note between the white ones. And, where the step required is just one semitone, the white notes have no black note between them. This gives the piano its characteristic appearance, with alternate groups of two and three black notes appearing at regular intervals among the white ones. In all other keys, both black and white notes must be used in order to play the scale. In the key of E major, for example, E (white) is doh. The next note, ray, must be two semitones up, which is the black note between F and G. This is called F sharp (F♯). You can work out the other notes in this and other major scales by simply following different patterns from the major scales, with one or more of the notes flattened (pitched down) by one semitone. In the key of C minor, the third note would be E flat (E♭).

Instruments such as the piano, with fixed, identical pitch changes between successive notes, are said to be *equally tempered.* As the frequency doubles over an octave, each of the twelve semitone steps must correspond to a frequency change of $\sqrt[12]{2}$ (the twelfth root of two), or 1.05946 times.

Harmonics

Most sound waves are complex mixtures of vibrations at various frequencies. The lowest frequency vibration is called the fundamental. Other vibrations, called harmonics, occur at whole-number multiples of the fundamental frequency. Figure A shows the combination of a 440 hertz fundamental with its second and third harmonics. The resultant complex wave has the same frequency as the fundamental and, therefore, the same pitch. But its harmonic content gives it a characteristic sound, quite different from that of the pure fundamental.

Figure B shows the relative levels of three components, and their positions in the sound frequency spectrum (range).

Concords and Discords

Playing two notes together sometimes produces a pleasing sound called a consonance, or *concord*. This happens when the frequencies of the notes are in some simple ratio to each other, such as 2:1 or 3:2. An unpleasant sound called a dissonance, or *discord*, occurs when frequencies are not related by such a simple ratio. For example, a discord is produced when two notes a semitone apart are played together.

Although the ratio between notes an octave apart is exactly 2:1, no other notes in the equally tempered scale are precisely related by a simple frequency ratio. For example, the frequency ratio between any sol and the doh below it is 1.498. However, this is very close to 1.500, or 3:2, and so a pleasant sound is heard when the two notes are played together. But a musician playing a violin, or some other instrument on which the intervals between the notes can be varied, could get the precise ratio of 3:2, and thus achieve a perfect blend of the two sounds. It is possible to tune a piano to a natural scale based on precise simple ratios between the frequencies of the various notes. This would produce perfect concords between certain notes, such as the first and fifth notes of the scale. But, on playing in a different key, the ratio between the new first and fifth notes would not be correct. And, in some keys the ratio would be so far out as to cause serious dissonance. The use of the equally tempered scale ensures that the frequency ratios are indentical in all keys and are close enough to their ideal values for most purposes.

Harmonics and Tone-Colour

Tone-colour, or timbre, is the quality that distinguishes the sound of one musical instrument from another. The sound vibrations produced by most musical instruments are extremely complex, being made up of numerous simple vibrations. The *fundamental*, or lowest-frequency vibration, gives the sound its characteristic pitch. Other vibrations, occurring at whole-number multiples of the fundamental frequency, modify the sound and give it its tone colour. These higher-frequency

Most musical instruments produce extremely complex sound waves containing many harmonics. Figure C shows the fundamental and harmonics produced when the note A is played on a piano.

Figure D shows the components of the same note as played on a violin. The fundamental is the same as before, so the note has the same pitch. But the harmonic content is different, which is why the two instruments sound very different.

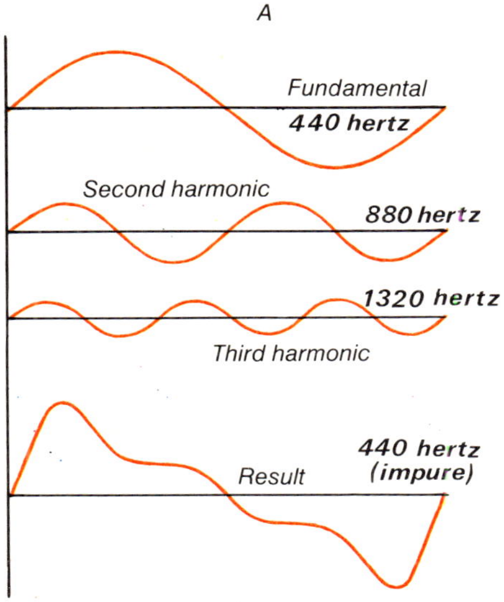

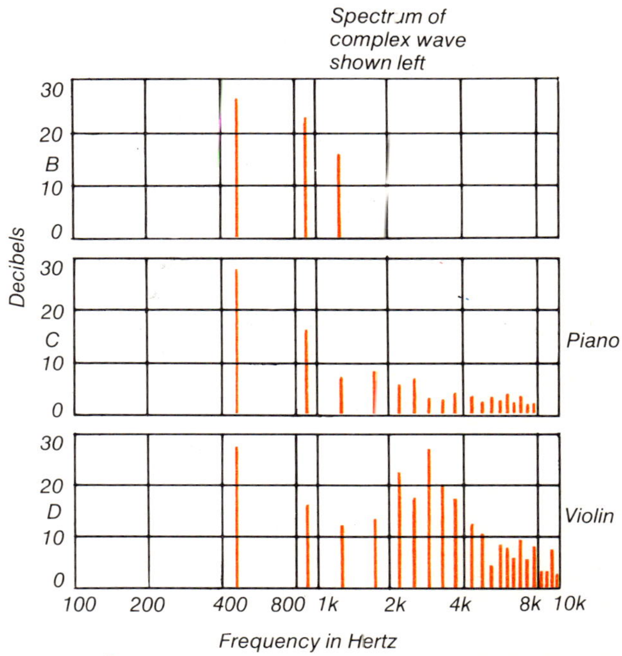

vibrations, called *harmonics*, are named according to their relationship to the fundamental. The third harmonic, for example, occurs at three times the fundamental frequency.

The construction of an instrument and the way it is played determine the harmonic content and, hence, the tone-colour of the notes. Most instruments produce a wide range of harmonics. The harmonics from a cello, for example, extend to beyond 10 kilohertz, although the instrument's fundamental frequency range ends around 700 hertz. For this reason, any recording or amplification equipment used for music must respond equally well to a wide range of frequencies if each instrument is to be reproduced faithfully. Some percussion instruments, such as cymbals, produce sound waves containing so many high-level harmonics that no definite pitch can be detected.

Transients

The beginning of a note is usually quite different from the sound that follows. For a relatively strong force is applied at first in order to start the vibrations. The vibrations may then be maintained by means of a smaller force, as in a wind instrument, or allowed to die away, as in the case of a bell. The waves produced at the brief initial stage of a note are called *transients*. Their harmonic content is quite different from the spectrum produced later, and has a marked effect on our assessment of the instrument's colour-tone. This can be demonstrated by first tape recording the same note played on a piano and a guitar. If the tape is then edited to remove the initial part of each note, they will be much more difficult to tell apart when the tape is replayed.

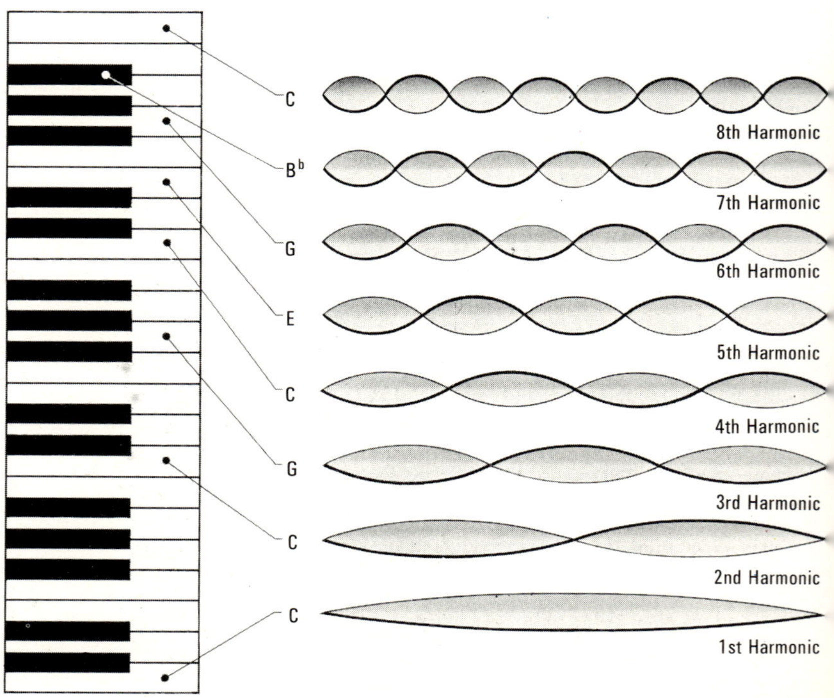

When a piano string vibrates it gives out a series of harmonics. These harmonics can be heard by holding down the keys shown, without sounding them, and then striking the bottom key sharply – in this case a C. The harmonics of this note will resonate.

In the Groove

In December 1877, a man walked into the offices of *Scientific American* magazine. He placed a small machine on one of the desks and turned a handle. To the astonishment of the office staff, the machine asked how they were feeling and if they liked the machine. The man was Thomas Alva Edison, and he called his machine the phonograph. For the first time, man was able to record and play back sound. As with many inventions, the principle of the phonograph was so simple that it seemed surprising that it had not been invented much earlier.

To make a recording, you had to speak into a small mouthpiece. This directed the sounds onto a thin iron disc called the diaphragm, making it vibrate. To the other side of the diaphragm was fixed a steel point, or stylus. This pressed against a layer of tin foil wrapped around a small horizontal cylinder mounted on a spindle. During recording, the handle was turned steadily about once per second. The spindle had a screw thread cut into it, so turning the handle made the cylinder rotate and move slowly sideways. As the cylinder moved, the steel point made a spiral groove in the soft tin foil, and the vibrations of the diaphragm caused variations in the depth of the groove. Thus the sound waves were impressed in the foil. After moving the diaphragm away from the foil, the cylinder was wound back to its original

Thomas Alva Edison poses for the camera with his tin foil phonograph in 1878. Edison regarded the phonograph as his favourite invention. It was certainly one of the most original inventions of all time.

Edison's original tin foil phonograph, invented in 1877. It consisted simply of a mouthpiece containing a thin iron diaphragm, on which was fixed a steel stylus. The stylus was made to run in grooves on a tin-foil-coated cylinder as the crank was turned. The recording was played back using a lighter parchment diaphragm.

position. The recording could then be played back using a lighter parchment diaphragm connected to a steel stylus. This was allowed to rest in the groove while the handle was turned once more. The variation in the depth of the groove made the steel point move up and down, causing the diaphragm to vibrate and emit sound. As the vibrations were a copy of the original vibrations used to make the recording, the original sound was reproduced. To increase the volume of the sound, a paper cone could be fitted over the parchment diaphragm. This acted like a simple megaphone.

Of course, the sound quality from this crude machine was far from perfect. But speech was clearly recognizable, and soon everyone wanted to hear the new gadget for themselves. One of the main problems with Edison's phonograph was that the tin foil recordings became scratched and extremely noisy after only a few playings. Better results were obtained in the 1880s by Chichester Bell and Charles Sumner. Their invention, which they called a gramophone, was patented in 1886. It worked in a similar way to Edison's machine, but used cylinders coated with wax instead of tin foil. The superior quality of this machine caused Edison to change over to wax cylinders. Another improvement introduced around this time was the use of a clockwork motor to turn the cylinder.

But, now that the novelty of recorded sound had started to wear off, public interest declined. To counteract this, Edison started to record well-known musicians. By 1890, recordings by various artists were on sale to the general public, and a whole new industry had been born. But already, an important new development was emerging—the disc gramophone.

Sound on Disc

In 1887, a German called Emile Berliner patented the first disc gramophone. At first recordings were made on a zinc disc coated with a smooth layer of wax. Later, a disc of vulcanite (hardened rubber) was used. The disc was placed on a horizontal turntable, which revolved when a handle was turned. As in the phonograph, a groove

The wax cylinder replaced the early Edison tin foil cylinder. It gave considerably improved results. Edison went on making cylinders until 1929, long after they had been replaced by the disc.

was cut by a steel stylus connected to a diaphragm vibrated by sound waves. But Berliner had introduced a most important change in technique. Instead of moving up and down as it cut the groove, the stylus moved from side to side. One problem with the up-and-down cylinder grooves had been that, on playback, the stylus tended to jump across from one "hill" to the next. As a result, the sound was not reproduced correctly, a great deal of background noise was produced and the grooves suffered considerable damage. On Berliner's machine, the constant groove depth avoided this problem. On playback, a needle in the wavy spiral groove reproduced the original vibrations. A diaphragm linked to the needle made the vibrations louder. And a large, trumpet-like horn amplified the sound further.

Berliner's gramophone was originally used as a children's toy. But, by chance, it came to have great commercial appeal. For, by 1898, a method had been found for mass producing recorded discs. An original disc could be used to make a metal plate, from which numerous copies could be pressed out on the machine—a process impossible with cylinders. The new technique meant that records of popular music could be supplied quickly to anyone who wanted them, and at a cheaper price. Previously, artists had to perform in front of several machines in order to make a small batch of records. And they had to repeat the process until the required number of discs had been cut. The introduction of record presses cut out this tedious business. And so, from that time, record production quickly grew to become a major industry.

To record an orchestra, the musicians would be seated around the mouth of a giant horn. This gradually tapered to a small diameter at the other end, where the diaphragm and cutting stylus were attached. Unfortunately, reflections of sounds within the horn gave the music an unnatural quality, rather like the sound you hear if you put your ear to a long length of scaffold tubing. Another problem with this early recording technique was that it was difficult to achieve a good sound balance when there were several instruments. Relatively quiet instruments, such as the guitar, could not be heard at all unless they were placed very close to the mouth of the horn. Once the players had been carefully positioned according to the power of their instruments, the recording session would begin. But no adjustment could be made if one of the musicians happened to play slightly louder or softer than normal. As a result, the sound balance was often unacceptable, and the recording had to be remade. This problem was overcome in the 1920s with the introduction of electric recordings.

The first gramophone developed by Emile Berliner in 1887. This was the first machine to use flat wax discs, turned by a hand crank. The same machine was used to record and replay sound. Recorded sound was amplified by the horn. This machine was the basis for all future acoustic gramophones.

Electric Recordings

All early sound recordings were purely acoustic. In other words, energy from the sound waves was itself used to move the cutter to make the variations in the groove. However, with the development of radio broadcasting in the early 1900s, recording techniques were destined to change. In the broadcasting studio, signals from microphones were amplified and mixed together, the combined signal then being fed to a transmitter. By using two or more microphones and carefully controlling the proportions in which their signals were mixed, the sound balance between various sources could be adjusted at will. For example, one microphone was used to pick up the sound of a piano, while a separate microphone was used for an accompanying singer. Controls associated with each microphone would be adjusted at the start of the performance and readjusted from time to time as necessary. In this way, the best balance between the two sounds could be maintained throughout the performance. And the singer's microphone could be turned right down when only the piano was playing. Doing this prevented unwanted breathing sounds from the singer interfering with the listener's enjoyment of the piano solo.

Such control over the sound signals was just what record companies wanted. If the signals from microphones could be mixed together and used to work an electric device for cutting a groove in a disc, their problems of controlling sound balance would be solved.

After an experimental period lasting about five years, a commercial system of electric recording was introduced in 1925. The principle was simplicity itself, yet the advantages were enormous. The signal to be recorded was amplified and fed to the disc cutter. There the signal passed through an electromagnet consisting of a small coil of wire free to move from side to side. Near the electromagnet was a permanent magnet, fixed in position. Changes in the strength and direction of the

Above: the "Puck" phonograph was made in Germany about 1900. Also known as the "Lyre", it was much cheaper then Edison's phonographs of the time, but it had no facilities for recording. It was powered by a single-spring clockwork motor.

The diagram below shows the basic parts of an electric cutting head.

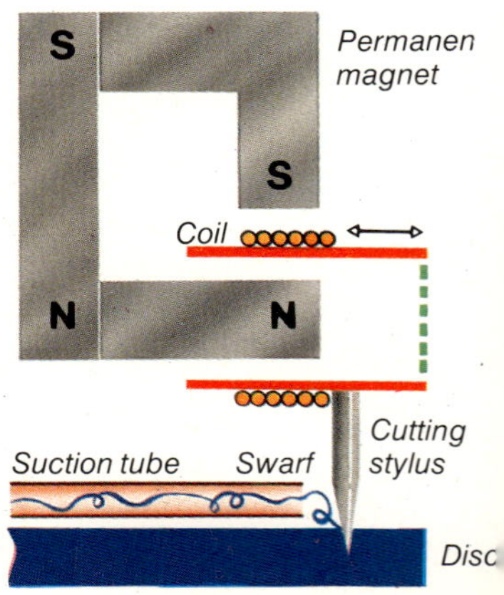

electric current passing through the coil made its magnetism vary. This caused it to be alternately attracted and repelled by the permanent magnet. The resultant side to side vibrations of the coil therefore resembled the vibrations of the sounds being recorded. Attached to the coil was a cutting stylus made of sapphire. This cut a wavy groove in the disc as it revolved. A screw mechanism made the cutter move slowly across the disc during recording. The result was a spiral groove starting at the outside and ending near the centre.

Besides giving much more control, use of the electric system resulted in recordings of far superior quality. For the resonance effects produced in the horn of the acoustic equipment were avoided. Some problems did occur with resonances in the electric cutting head. But these were relatively easy to overcome.

So far, we have considered only the control of sound volume during recording. But, once a sound signal has been converted to an electric one by a microphone, electronic circuits can be used to apply various other forms of control. The most important of these are bass and treble controls. Some types of control allow the recording engineer simply to cut the bass or treble content of the sound signal by a fixed or variable amount. Other types also enable the signal to be boosted at these frequencies. If a recording is made in a room that is not well insulated from external sounds, bass cut can be used to reduce the low frequency rumble of passing traffic. Treble cut can be used to reduce the harsh sibilant quality of some voices. Another use of bass and treble controls is as an artificial means of changing the apparent quality of the sounds produced by various instruments. In a modern recording studio, many kinds of electronic control are provided.

Early gramophones have become collectors' pieces, to be preserved with loving care. On the left is one of the first disc machines. With it are boxes of "loud" and "soft" steel needles. The well-preserved model on the right took wax cylinders called "records".

In the early days of electric recording, performers had to contend with rather primitive equipment. This photograph, taken in 1930, shows the film star Pola Negri making her first recording at the Queen's Hall in London.

Playing Records

When the first electric disc recording system was introduced, the record-buying public were equipped with gramophones based on Emile Berliner's invention. These ranged from bulky models with enormous horns, to small, portable types. The gramophone horn was connected to a device called the sound box. This contained the diaphragm and a holder for the needle that followed the record groove. Portables, and most of the larger models were operated by a clockwork motor, which was wound by turning a handle. If you did not wind it up enough the record would slow down while it was playing. This caused the tempo and pitch of the music to decrease until the sounds became almost unrecognizable and the record finally came to a halt. Although some models were fitted with an electric motor, not everyone had an elecricity supply connected to their home. So the clockwork gramophone remained popular for some time.

A few gramphones were fitted with small doors over the open end of the horn. If you wanted to reduce the volume of sound, you simply closed the doors. Unfortunately, this also changed the quality of the sound produced, but it did avoid upsetting the neighbours late at night. On a gramophone without this refinement, you could get a similar effect by stuffing an old sock or some other garment up the horn. Another method of controlling volume on acoustic gramophones was to select an appropriate type of playing needle. Thick, "loud tone" needles gave most volume, as they formed a fairly rigid link between the groove and diaphragm. Thinner, more flexible, "soft tone" needles were used when less volume was required.

The first all-electric gramophone appeared in the United States in 1925—the same year that electric recordings were introduced. Instead of a diaphragm and horn, it had an electric pickup, amplifier and loudspeaker. The pickup converted vibrations of the needle into an electric signal that varied in the same way as the sound waves recorded on the disc. The signal was then amplified and fed to the loudspeaker, which reproduced it as sound. A control on the amplifier enabled the volume to be adjusted as required without affecting the sound quality. Over the years, many inventors and engineers helped to improve the quality of records and gramophones, which eventually became known as record players. But the acoustic, wind-up machine remained popular for many years, especially the smaller portable models. Some were still produced as late as the 1950s, although sales had decreased considerably. By that time, high quality, long-playing discs were being produced in large quantities, and they had to be played using light-weight pickups. So the days of the wind-up gramophone, with its heavy sound box, were numbered.

Although electric recording was introduced in 1925, the late 1920s still saw enormous horns attached to acoustic gramophones.

Quality, Speed and Duration

Most of the gramophone records produced in the 1920s were made of shellac mixed with slate dust and carbon particles to increase hardness. The use of these materials, called fillers, was necessary in order to reduce record wear. But it also gave the disc a rough surface that produced a great deal of background hiss when played. Another problem was the relatively short playing time. The popular ten-inch diameter record lasted no more than four minutes per side. And the use of twelve-inch records only extended the maximum playing time to just over five minutes. So most artists restricted themselves to recording short pieces. Longer works had to be recorded on a set of records, and the listener had the tedious and distracting task of continually changing and turning over the records.

The record industry was, therefore, faced with the urgent problem of extending the playing time of records without any deterioration in sound quality. There were many possibilities, but every approach presented new problems. The simplest way of extending the playing time of the record was to increase its diameter. This had been done as early as 1904, when the first long-playing records, measuring 20 inches in diameter, were produced in London. But, to accommodate these huge discs, much bigger gramophones were required. This would have made equipment for the home unacceptably large. And portable gramophones for the twenty-inch disc would have been quite out of the question.

An alternative solution to the problem of record duration was to use discs of standard size with much finer grooves. In this way, the number of grooves across the disc, and hence the playing time, could be increased considerably. The problem here was that, as the grooves were much closer together, the amount by which they could deviate from side to side was greatly reduced. As a result, the volume of the recorded sound was reduced too, while the background hiss from the disc remained unchanged. In technical terms, this is described as a worsening of the signal-to-noise ratio. In practical terms, it meant that the high background noise on the discs became much more distracting. The way to solve this problem was to make the discs from a material that gave less background noise. The first step was to do away with fillers, as these were the main cause of the noise. But this made the discs too soft to be used with the pickups in common use at that time. After only a few playings, the discs would have been so badly scratched that the noise would have been much higher, not lower, than with conventional materials. This was avoided by replacing the standard pickup with one of light-weight design.

Most pickups on early gramophones used steel needles. So it may, at first, seem strange that, with softer discs, an even harder material had to be used for the needle, or stylus. Although hard, the rounded tips of steel needles soon lost their shape when playing records. And even the slightest flattening of the tip would damage the groove of a soft disc. Therefore, for such records, a stylus made from a gem stone, such as diamond or sapphire, was used. These materials could be cut and polished to produce an extremely smooth, round tip of the required radius.

Long-playing fine-groove discs, now referred to as microgroove recordings, were first issued in 1926 by the Edison Company. They played at a speed of 80 rpm, (revolutions per minute) as this was before the standard of 78 rpm had become generally accepted. The discs, measuring ten or twelve inches in diameter, were made of a substance called phenolic, the larger size giving a maximum playing time of about 20 minutes per side. Instead of the normal 100 grooves to the inch, the Edison discs had about 450. Unfortunately, the thin walls of the grooves were too fragile, and the playing stylus would sometimes break through to the next groove, causing a sudden jump in the music. Although this project was a failure, it did establish principles that were later to play an important part in the development of the long-playing record.

Yet another way of increasing the playing time of a disc was to record and play back at a lower speed. But this, too, presented a problem. For the cutter did not work so well as when the disc was moving fast, especially at high frequencies. Trying to cut a groove in a slow-moving disc was rather like trying to plane a piece of wood extremely slowly. The cutter tended to stick. To overcome this effect, a small electric heating coil was placed around the cutting stylus. The hot tip warmed the surface of the disc, making it quite easy to cut.

The first low-speed long-playing records were issued in 1931 in the United States by the RCA-Victor Company. These standard-size

In 1942, when this photograph was taken, broadcasting companies still made recordings on 78 rpm shellac discs. The commercial use of tape recording was still a long way off.

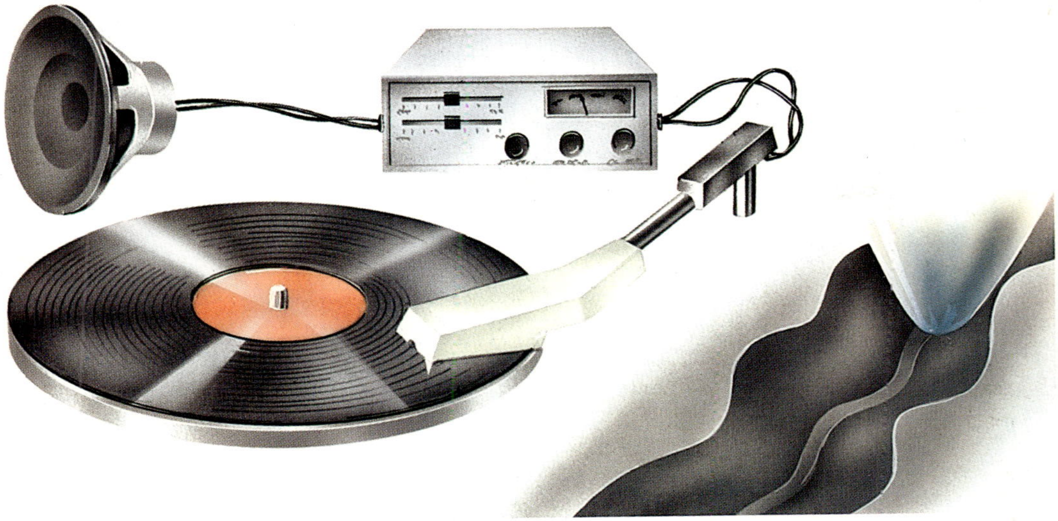

Until the early 1950s the standard record was still a mono disc played at 78 rpm. Quality was, however, quite good, with crystal styluses and electric amplification and volume control.

microgroove discs turned at 33 rpm and, therefore, required special playback equipment. This, too, could be bought from the record company. But the price was far too much for the average person to pay, and so the enterprise failed. However, it had demonstrated that low-speed disc recording was a practical proposition. And the speed used by RCA-Victor eventually became the standard speed for long-playing records.

The real breakthrough in this field came in 1948, when Columbia issued a series of 33 rpm long-playing discs. These microgroove recordings were made of vinylite with about 250 grooves per inch, giving a playing time of over 20 minutes per side. Columbia's new discs quickly became popular. They gave high quality sound, and reasonably priced playing equipment was available. To satisfy the rapidly rising demand for long-playing records, other companies soon went into production.

By the 1950s, the business was booming. RCA introduced the seven-inch 45 rpm microgroove single as an alternative to the ten-inch 78 rpm record. The seven-inch format was also used for EPs—extended play records containing the equivalent of two single records. For a time, most record players were produced with speeds of 78, 45 and 33 rpm. Usually, the pickup was fitted with two styli of different sizes. One was used for 78 rpm records, and the other for the microgroove recordings. Sales of the 45 rpm records soon exceeded those of the 78s and, within a few years, production of the latter had virtually ceased. As a result, more and more record players were produced having only two speeds—45 and 33 rpm. This meant that pickup design could be simplified too, as only one stylus was required. However, other complications were arising. For, by that time, high-fidelity and stereophonic records had appeared, and these led to a demand for various refinements in record-playing equipment.

High Fidelity Records

Striving to obtain the best possible sound quality, Decca introduced high-fidelity records in 1944. The company used the term "full frequency range recording" to describe their new system, which worked over the range 50 to 14,000 hertz. Although not actually covering the full sound frequency range, the Decca discs were a great improvement on earlier commercial records. So the description high-fidelity, or hi-fi for short, was a fair one. It meant that, with suitable equipment, the reproduced sound would be a good copy of the original. At first, only a few enthusiasts enjoyed the advantages of high fidelity. Most people had record players quite incapable of clearly reproducing the full range of frequencies on these discs. But manufacturers were quick to respond to the demand for better equipment, and soon a wide range was available. People with sufficient money could buy a high-quality sound system. And less wealthy enthusiasts learned how to improve their existing equipment by building better amplifiers and carefully designed loudspeaker cabinets. (High quality sound reproduction systems are described on page 56.)

Digital Recording
Gramophone records are normally made by copying a master tape prepared in a studio. As a result, tape hiss can often be heard on the record. One way of overcoming this problem is to use digital recording techniques in the studio. All the sounds are converted into a code of electrical pulses, which are recorded on the tape. On replay, these pulses are reconverted into normal analog sound signals. In this process, circuits sense the presence or absence of pulses, but are unaffected by the tape hiss. The hiss-free sound signals produced are then copied onto disc in the normal way.

Stereophonic Records

Sound reproduction through a single loudspeaker is called monophonic. Although the quality may be superb, it is unnatural to hear all sounds coming from exactly the same position. In real life, a group of musicians would be spread out, the sounds of their instruments reaching us from various directions. And, even when we listen to a person speaking, we hear reflections of the voice from various parts of the room—although we are not always aware of it. In its simplest form, stereophonic sound recording is an attempt to present us with sounds as we would hear them in real life. Two microphones are used to pick up the sounds that our two ears would hear. The two sound signals can be recorded on a disc and later replayed through two loudspeakers placed about three metres apart, to give a reasonable illusion of reality. Sounds seem to come from various positions between the speakers, and you can often sense whether the recording was made in a large hall or in a small studio. It must, however, be emphasised that this is an example of the simplest possible stereophonic recording technique. As we shall see when we deal with professional sound recording in detail, more complex techniques are normally used to produce the two stereo signals.

The photographs below give an enlargement of 50 times. That on the left shows the grooves of a mono shellac disc. On the right is a 33 rpm vinyl stereo disc, in which the different tracks on either side of each groove can be clearly seen.

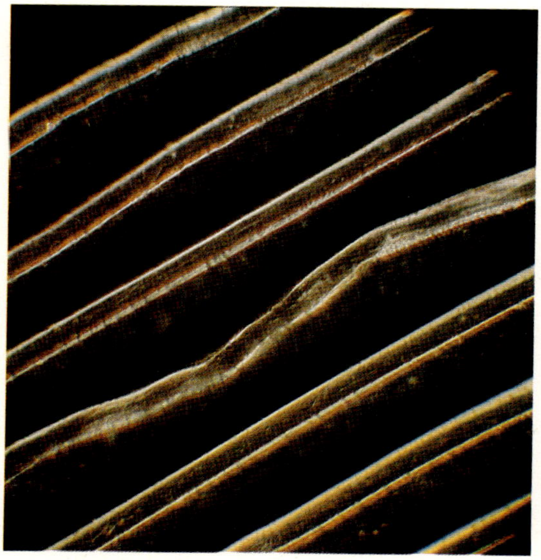

Two into One

A major difficulty in the development of stereophonic discs was in finding a way of recording the two signals separately. A fairly obvious solution was to cut the grooves side by side, using a double cutting head. This system was tried out in the 1940s. For reproduction, a double pickup head with two styli was lowered onto the record. But, half the time, the styli would end up in the wrong grooves, so that one picked up the signal one turn ahead of the other. Also, the playing time was halved by cutting two grooves instead of one.

In the mid 1950s, a system was devised whereby both signals could be recorded in a single groove. The two signals were used to make a single cutting stylus move in different directions—up and down and from side to side. On replay, a pickup with a single stylus converted these movements back into two separate signals. Although satisfactory stereophonic sound could be obtained by this method, the quality of the up-and-down channel was never as good as the one recorded in the normal manner. The solution was to use the two signals to make the stylus cut different shapes in each side of the single groove. As with the previous system, a special pickup converted the two components of movement into separate signals for reproduction on a pair of loudspeakers. This system was used for the first commercial stereophonic discs, which were issued in the United States in 1958 by Audio Fidelity. And it is the system we still use today.

A disc-cutting engineer examines a "master lacquer" before recording. It is from this disc that all other versions of the recording will be made.

Making a Record

The recording, on a stereo master tape, is copied onto a lacquer disc (left). The groove made by the disc-cutting lathe can be nearly a kilometre long. Sound signals from the tape make the cutting stylus vibrate. The left and right signals are each recorded as a wavy track in one wall of the groove.

The master lacquer produced is inspected to make sure that it is free from flaws (below left). It is not played, as this would damage the soft lacquer.

The master lacquer has been given a fine coating of silver. It is now placed in an electroplating bath, where it will receive a nickel coating (below).

The lacquer is now pulled away from the nickel master that has formed (above). This is a negative replica of the lacquer, with ridges instead of grooves.

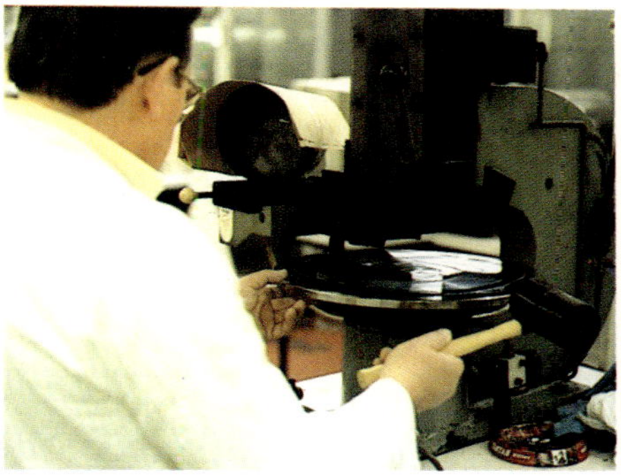

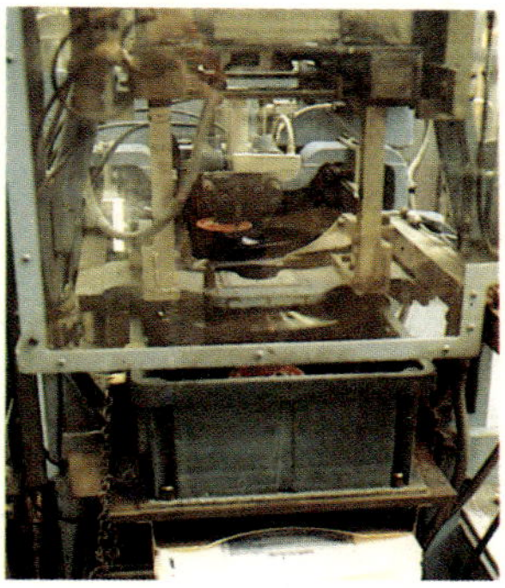

The nickel master is coated with a chemical film. On this is plated another layer of nickel. The film separating the two nickel discs allows the "working positive" formed to be separated from the master. Like the original lacquer, the positive has grooves. Here it is being cleaned (top right).

The positive is used in another plating process to produce a nickel matrix, or stamper. The optical centring machine shown here accurately locates the middle of the stamper, where it pierces a hole (centre left).

An automatic press places the record labels and hot vinyl material between two stampers. It then presses them together to form a double-sided record (centre right). After pressing, the discs are inspected and then packed for distribution (right).

Sound on Tape

In 1898, a Danish telephone engineer called Valdemar Poulsen invented a new method for recording sound. He converted it into a magnetic pattern on a length of piano wire. To do this, Poulsen passed the signal from a microphone through an electromagnet—a coil of wire, wound on an iron core. The wire was drawn past this electromagnet, which acted as a recording and reproduction head. Variations in the strength and frequency of sounds entering the microphone made the current through the head vary in a similar way. This caused corresponding changes in the strength of the magnetism produced. So, as the wire passed the head, it acquired a pattern of magnetization. To replay this recording, the wire was first rewound and then drawn past the head again. This time, a pair of headphones was connected to the head. Now, when a coil of wire is subjected to a changing magnetic field, an electrical voltage is produced across the coil. So the variations in the wire's magnetic strength produced corresponding voltage variations in the head. And the headphones converted these variations back into sounds.

Poulsen's machine, called the Telegraphone, was used as an office dictation machine and also to record telephone messages. But the recordings were of poor quality, and the volume too weak for it to become a commercial success.

The first tape recorder was Louis Blattner's Blattnerphone of 1929. Like Poulsen's machine, it recorded sound as magnetic patterns, but used steel tape that was wound on huge spools. Electronic valves amplified the signals going to and from the machine, which was used originally to record film sound tracks at Elstree, England.

Plastic tape, coated with a layer of magnetic iron oxide, first appeared in Germany in 1935. This had one great advantage over steel tape—it was easy to cut and stick together. This meant that unwanted parts of a recording could be quickly removed. And new material could be inserted at any point along the tape. But one problem still to be overcome was the high background hiss that could be heard on the recordings. During the next ten years, the Germans made great advances in tape recording technology and largely overcame this problem. When the war ended in 1945, the Allied Forces were highly impressed by the Magnetophon tape recorders they discovered in Berlin. As a result, all further developments in tape recording in the United States, Britain and France used this machine as a starting point. And, in spite of numerous improvements and refinements made since those days, the basic principles of magnetic tape recording remain unchanged.

Professional Tape Recorders

Professional tape recorders are often much simpler than those made for home use. For example, in a recording studio, you will not find any bass or treble controls on the recorders. Any tone adjustment would

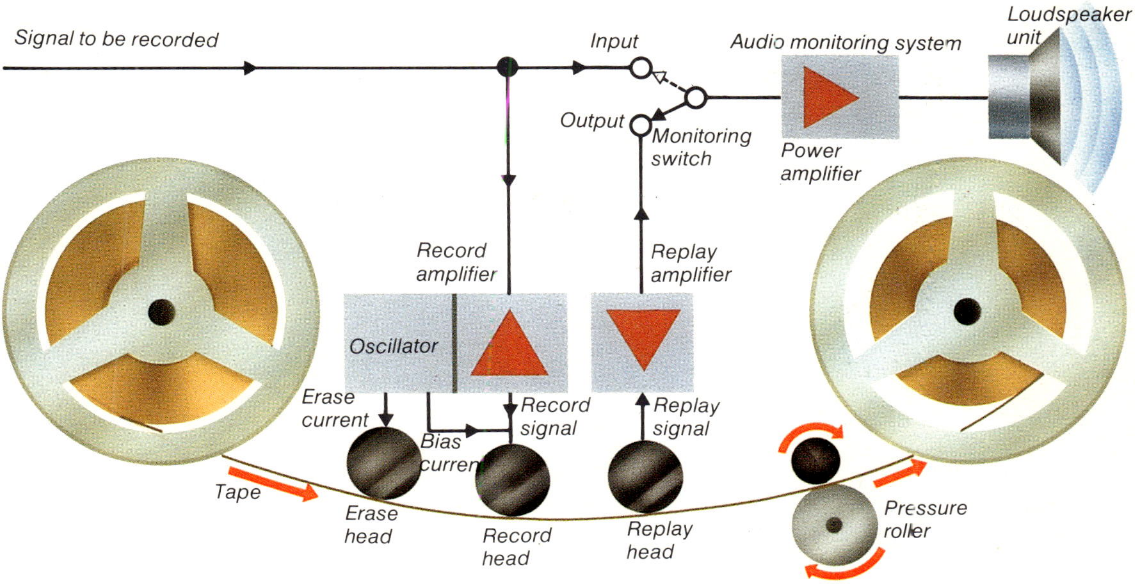

be carried out on the engineer's control desk. Also, any mixing of signals would be done using controls on the desk. So, in its simplest form, the professional tape machine can merely record and reproduce suitable sound signals, and erase any previously recorded material on a tape. For convenience, there may be a small loudspeaker in the machine. But, for normal playback, a separate monitoring system, consisting of a power amplifier and high quality loudspeaker unit would be used.

The basic machine has three heads for erase, record, and replay (playback). These are connected to the record and replay amplifiers. During recording and replay, the tape is moved past the heads at a constant speed. This is controlled by a spindle called the capstan. It rotates at a set speed, and the tape is pressed against it by a rubber wheel called the pressure roller. When winding forward or back, the roller moves away from the tape so that it can pass through the machine at high speed.

The diagram above shows the layout of a basic tape recorder.

Magnetic particles on tape before recording

Magnetic particles on tape after recording

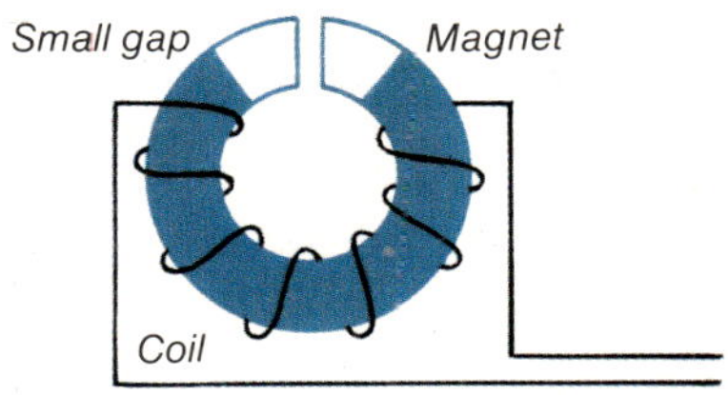

The tape is coated with iron oxide, the particles in which behave like tiny magnets. When the tape passes the recording head (above) the magnetic particles in the tape become lined up in strong or weak magnetic patterns as commanded by the signal passing through the recording head. The gap in the magnet of the head is very small to ensure maximum magnetic force.

A close-up of part of a professional tape recorder. A high level of precision is required in the manufacture of such equipment. It is vital that the tape always passes the heads at an exact angle.

The manufacture of plastic tape is now a major industry. In the top picture, large rolls of tape are being polished. The polished tape is then coated with iron oxide and stored (centre). In the bottom picture, the coated tape is being slit into cassette width, 0.15 inches (3.8 mm).

The most common type of tape used today is made of plastic, coated with a layer of magnetic iron oxide. In this layer, the particles of oxide act as tiny magnets. Like compass needles, they will swing around when influenced by a nearby magnet. However, if the magnet is then removed, the particles will remain pointing in their new directions. In a blank tape, the particles point in random directions, and the tape has no overall magnetization.

To ensure that the tape is blank before recording on it, a strong current is passed through the erase head. This current is alternating—moving first one way and then the other. The changing magnetic force produced in the erase head makes the particles in the tape coating swing rapidly to and fro. As a result, any magnetic patterns formed by previous recording are destroyed. As the tape moves away from the erase head, the effect gets weaker, and the particles eventually end up in random positions. The tape is thus erased and ready to have a new magnetic pattern imposed on it at the record head.

During recording, the electric signals passing through the record head make it act as a magnet of varying strength. A strong signal through the head will pull the particles in the passing tape so that they all point in the same direction. And, when the tape has passed the head, the particles remain lined up. With all their north poles pointing in one direction, and their south poles in the opposite direction, their magnetic forces now act together to produce a detectable magnetization of the tape. Weaker signals passing through the record head produce a similar effect, except that fewer particles are brought into line, resulting in a weaker magnetic pattern being left on the tape. In this way, within certain limits, every variation in the signal passing through the record head is recorded on the tape.

When the tape is played back, the magnetic pattern induces an electrical signal in the replay head. This signal is strengthened in the replay amplifier, and then fed to the power amplifier and loudspeaker unit, where it is reproduced as sound.

An important feature of the machine described here is that the replay facility can be used while a recording is being made. Usually, the monitoring system can be switched either to the signal entering the record amplifier, or to the signal leaving the replay amplifier. This allows the studio engineer to check the quality of a recording while it is being made. If, for example, he hears distortion of the replayed signal, he would switch his monitoring system to check the incoming signal. If that sounds satisfactory, then he knows that the recorder is faulty. But, if the incoming signal sounds distorted too, then the fault must lie between the sound source and the recorder. This technique of checking a tape as it is being recorded is common in sound broadcasting studios, where it is often vital to detect and locate faults as soon as possible. It would, for example, be disastrous to record a whole concert, only to discover afterwards that the recording was faulty.

Bias

For a sound to be recorded accurately, the magnetism remaining on the tape must be proportional to the current passed through the record head. Unfortunately, these two quantities are not proportional when the current is very small. So, in order to avoid excessive distortion in the recording, this problem must be overcome. To do this, an additional current, known as the *bias*, is added to the signal to be recorded. Then, even with a small signal, the total current through the record head is relatively high, and the magnetism on the tape is proportional to the signal strength. A direct current—one that flows always in the same direction—could be used for the bias. But much better results are obtained using an alternating current—one that flows first one way and then the other. The frequency of this

Sound is recorded on tape as a magnetic pattern. During recording, a strong, rapidly alternating current passes through the erase head. The changing magnetic field produced destroys any previously recorded pattern on the tape, leaving it unmagnetized. The signals to be recorded are passed through the record head. This magnetizes the passing tape, leaving on it a pattern corresponding to the sound signals. The tape's magnetic pattern produces a sound signal in the replay head. This signal is amplified and reproduced on a loudspeaker. Professional machines often have a separate replay head like this, so that the recording can be checked as it is being made. This is not possible on most domestic recorders, which have one head for both recording and replay.

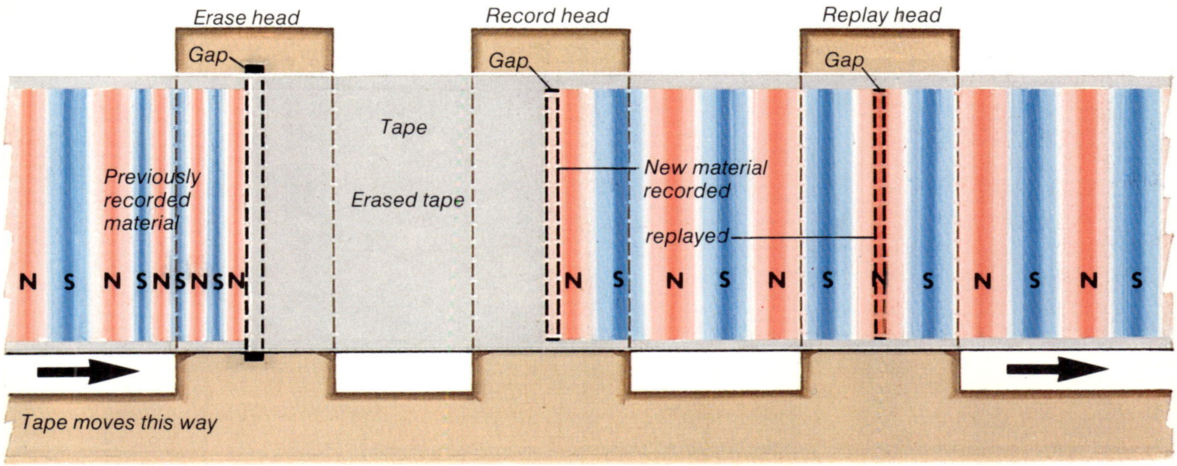

Plastic tape is coated with a layer of magnetic iron oxide. This photograph shows the striped magnetic pattern in the coating of parts of the tape on which sound has been recorded. The magnetic pattern is made visible to the camera by using cadmium powder.

alternating current has to be above the audible range, otherwise it would be heard as a note superimposed on the recording. In practice, a frequency of about 100kHz is often used. It is generated by a part of the record amplifier called the oscillator. This high-frequency supply is also used to provide the current for the erase head.

Controlling the Level

Tape produces a characteristic hiss that can be heard behind the recording. This will be most noticeable when material is recorded at a low level. For the volume will have to be turned up on replay. This will bring the reproduced sounds up to a reasonable level. But, at the same time, the level of tape hiss will increase too. For this reason, low recording levels should be avoided as far as possible. However, if the recording level is too high, the recording will be distorted. This occurs when the tape approaches saturation—maximum magnetization. Then, further increases in the recording current no longer result in similar increases in tape magnetization, and so distortion occurs. Another problem is that very high level sounds recorded on tape tend to "print through" to the next layer when the tape is wound onto the spool. One layer magnetizes the next, producing a faint, but distinct copy of the sounds.

Careful control of the recording level is, therefore, required in order to avoid these problems. Low-level passages must be increased in level so that they are recorded well above tape hiss level. And high-level passages must be brought down to avoid distortion and print through. A meter on the studio control desk indicates the sound level, and a control is adjusted throughout the recording to keep the level within the required limits.

Equalization

During the recording process, losses occur at high frequencies. There are two main causes. The tape head becomes less efficient and,

The Dolby System
The Dolby noise reduction system is designed to reduce the level of noise produced in any sound transmission or recording system. Without the use of Dolby, a background hiss is often heard, especially when a low level of sound is recorded on the tape. In the Dolby system, the signals to be recorded are first fed through an encoding circuit. The encoder boosts the low level sounds, leaving the high level sounds as they were. The encoded signals are then recorded in the normal way. As before, background noise appears behind the recorded signals. But now, the signals are fed through a Dolby decoding circuit. This reduces the previously boosted low level signals to their correct value. As the circuit does not distinguish between wanted and unwanted sounds, the low level noise signals are reduced too. So the recorded sounds are now at their correct levels, but the background noise is considerably less than before. The Dolby system is now widely used in both professional and domestic tape recording equipment.

therefore, produces a smaller magnetizing force for the same current. And the signal recorded on the tape tends to demagnetize itself. This occurs because the quickly changing current through the record head results in a series of tightly packed magnetic patches being formed on the tape. As the north and south poles on the tape are so close together, their opposite magnetic effects tend to cancel one another. As a result, the strength of the magnetic pattern left on the tape is decreased. To overcome these losses, the record amplifier is designed to boost the high frequencies by just the right amount. This ensures that the tape can be properly magnetized over a wide range of frequencies. The technique of compensating for losses at certain frequencies is called *equalization*.

On playback, equalization of a different kind is required. The signal produced in the replay head depends on the strength of the magnetic pattern on the tape. But it depends also on the rate at which the pattern changes as it passes the head. The rapidly changing pattern of a high-frequency note will produce a much stronger signal than will the slower changing pattern of a low frequency note, even though both are recorded on the tape at the same strength. To compensate for this effect, the replay amplifier must have an output that decreases as the frequency of the signal rises.

However, a second factor has also to be taken into account. In the replay head's metal core is a narrow gap where the magnetic effect of the tape is detected. Each passing north or south pole temporarily magnetizes the head and causes a voltage to appear across it. But, at some high frequency, the north and south poles of each magnetic patch will be so close together that they will be in the head gap at the same time. Their effects will then cancel, and no signal will appear across the head. The frequency at which this occurs is called the *extinction frequency*. Its value depends on the physical size of the replay head gap, and on the tape speed. Halving the gap, or doubling the tape speed will double the extinction frequency and thus usefully extend the frequency range over which satisfactory recordings can be made. However, the output from the replay head will still decrease as the extinction frequency is approached. So the upper frequencies are boosted on replay to compensate for this effect. The overall equalization for playback therefore gives an output that decreases steadily over most of the frequency range, and then rises again at the high frequency end.

The combined effect of record and replay equalization is to ensure that the system is capable of recording with consistent quality over a wide range of frequencies. If a tape machine has more than one running speed, then each will require different equalization. The necessary electronic components are usually switched into the amplifier circuits automatically according to the setting of the tape speed switch.

Multitrack Recording

Many professional tape machines record one track of sound along a tape 1/4 inch (6.3 mm) wide at a speed of 15 inches (38 centimetres) per second. If stereophonic sound is to be recorded, then extra amplifiers and special heads are used to record a pair of tracks along the tape. Such machines are commonly used in sound broadcasting studios.

In studios used mainly for recording music, machines capable of recording 4, 8, 16 or even more tracks on a tape are common. The speed is the same as before, but wider tape is used. Sixteen track recordings, for example, are usually made on tape 2 inches (50.8 mm) wide. With such a machine, each instrument in a group can be recorded on a separate track, with the lead singer and backing group on their own tracks too. If everything is satisfactory, except for a wrong note by one musican, that person can record his track again while listening to the sounds on the other tracks. In many cases, the singers record their tracks at a later session, and do not even have to meet the instrumentalists. Multitrack work thus provides great flexibility and allows changes to be made long after the original recording sessions. When these tracks have been perfected, the tape is replayed and the sounds mixed together in two groups. These form the two sound signals of a so-called stereophonic recording, although no stereophonic techniques may have been used. These two signals are copied onto a two-track master tape. Various effects, such as artificial reverberations, can be added to any of the sounds at this stage. The final stereo master tape is then sent to a factory for transfer onto disc or tape cassette. Most "stereophonic" recordings are now produced in this way. But true stereophonic effects can be obtained only by using one or more *pairs* of microphones placed in suitable positions so that they pick up sounds resembling those heard by our two ears.

Home Tape Equipment

To obtain the best quality recordings, a high tape speed is required. This is why professional recorders usually run at 15 inches (38 cm) per second. The keenest amateurs usually compromise by recording at a tape speed of 7.5 inches (19 cm) per second, with two or four tracks on a reel of 1/4 inch (6.3 mm) tape. This provides reasonably high quality, while being considerably cheaper than if professional standards were adopted. However, for most people, the standard cassette—the Musicassette, introduced by Philips in 1963—provides adequate quality. And it is so much more convenient. You merely push the

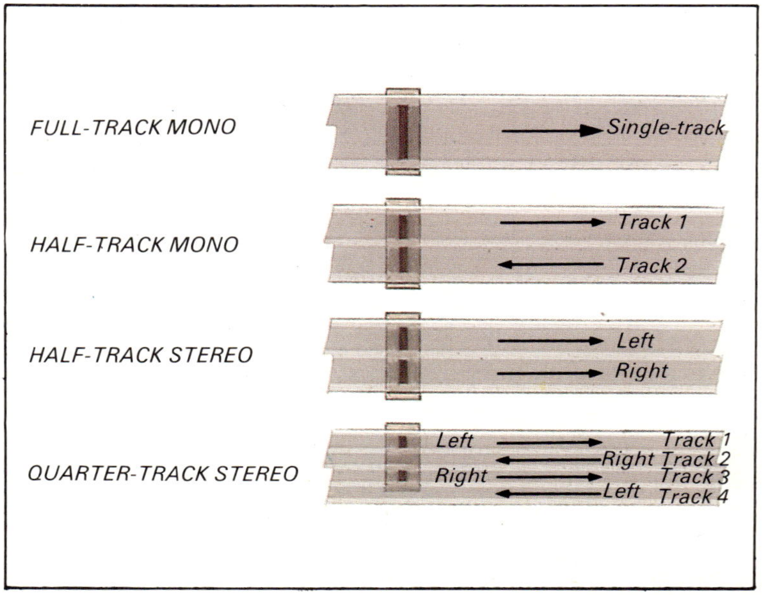

The most common open-reel recorders use 1/4-inch tape running at 1 7/8, 3 3/4, 7 1/2 or 15 inches per second. The diagram shows the tracks recorded along the tape by various types of machine. Many professional recorders use a single track spanning most of the tape width. With the half-track mono system after recording one track, the tape can be turned over to record another track in the other direction. Each tape, therefore, lasts twice as long as with the full-track system, but there is a slight reduction in sound quality. Similarly, the quarter-track stereo system gives twice the running time obtainable with the half-track stereo system. But, again, the sound quality is slightly impaired.

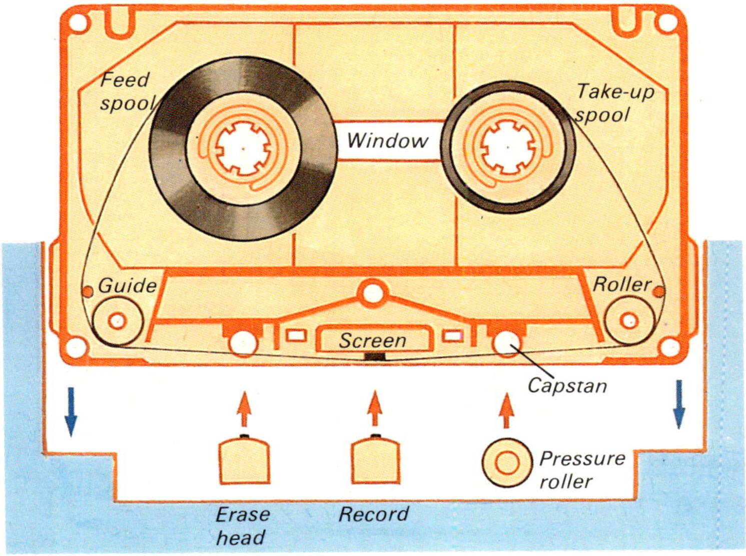

The Philips Compact Cassette system uses tape 0.15 inch wide, running at a speed of $1^7/_8$ inches per second. The recorder's capstan passes through a hole in the cassette. When the machine is switched to replay or record, the heads and pressure roller move towards the cassette. The tape is now gripped between the turning capstan and the pressure roller, and so is pulled past the heads. The right-hand spool turns gently to take up the tape. Close contact between the tape and the record/replay head is ensured by the pressure pad. The metal screen shields the head from stray magnetic fields that could otherwise produce hum during playback. The tape can be observed through a window provided in each side of the plastic cassette.

cassette into the machine, and it is ready to use. With separate reels of tape, threading the end through the machine takes much longer.

Cassettes run at a speed of only $1^7/_8$ inches (4.8 cm) per second, and use thin tape so that a reasonable length can be accommodated. Most cassettes have a total running time of 60 minutes, although up to 120 minutes is possible with extra-thin tape. The tape, which is only 0.15 inches (3.8 mm) wide accommodates two mono tracks, or two pairs of stereo tracks. After the tape has passed through the machine in one direction, the cassette is turned over so that the other track or tracks can then be used.

On the more expensive cassette machine, a noise reduction system is provided to reduce the tape hiss, which otherwise tends to be rather high. The hiss can be further reduced by using special low-noise "chrome" or "metal" tapes. But this is possible only if the recorder can provide the higher bias levels required by these tapes.

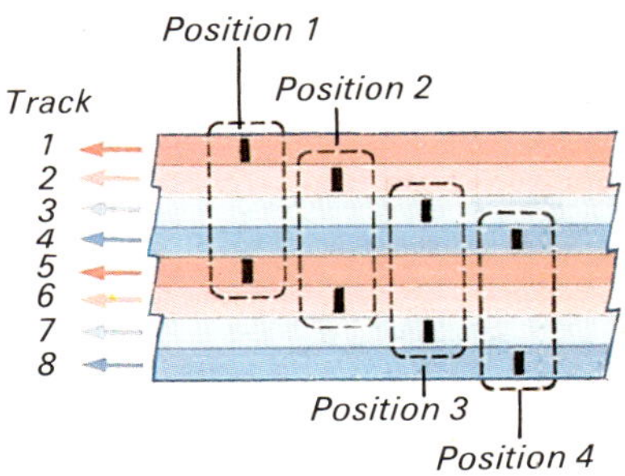

Cartridge machines are used mainly for playing pre-recorded tapes of background music. The ends of the cartridge tape are joined to form a long loop. This is contained on a single spool. The tape is pulled from the inside of the reel at a speed of $3^3/_4$ inches per second, and is wound back on the outside. The tape's eight tracks contain four stereo recordings. The replay head is moved across the tape in order to select the required tracks.

Home Hi-fi

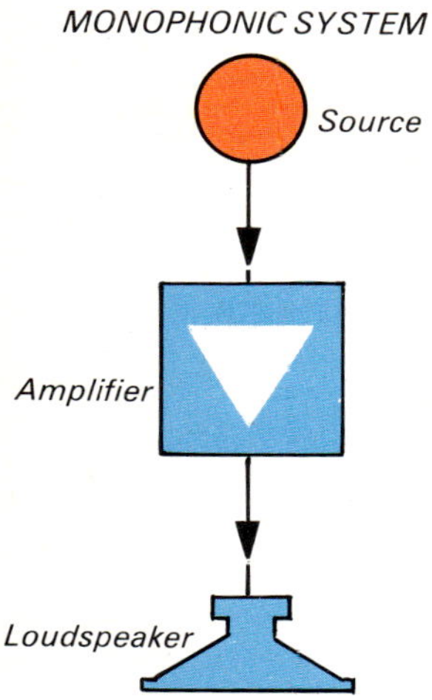

In a monophonic, or single-channel sound system, a signal is amplified and then reproduced on a single loudspeaker unit. The source of the signal may be a record deck, tape deck or radio tuner. In a stereophonic or two-channel system, the source produces a pair of sound signals from a stereo recording or transmission. These two signals are amplified separately and reproduced in a pair of loudspeakers.

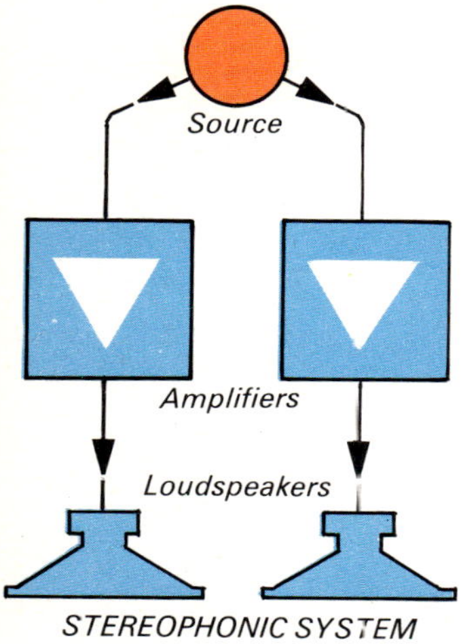

Trying to decide which is the best sound equipment for the home is a difficult task. There are so many makes and types of radio, record, tape and amplification equipment that even the experts have difficulty making a choice. Most manufacturers of domestic sound equipment supply technical information about their equipment. But this may be inaccurate, misleading, meaningless or not particularly important. And you cannot expect the manufacturer to tell you about any bad points his equipment may have. So it is much better to rely on the opinions of reviewers. You can read their reports on new equipment that they have tested in the numerous hi-fi magazines published each month. However, before trying to choose equipment, you need first to make some basic decisions.

Mono, Stereo or Quad?

The simplest sound reproduction system consists of three basic items: a source, such as a radio tuner, tape deck or record deck; an amplifier; and a loudspeaker. These form a simple monophonic (one-channel) sound system. A cheap portable radio, for example, contains all three items in one small case. The sound quality from such a set is often very poor. Usually the loudspeaker is the main cause. For good quality reproduction, it should be mounted in a properly designed cabinet with rigid walls. And resonances inside the cabinet must be reduced as much as possible by a sound-absorbent lining. The loudspeaker and its cabinet are referred to as a loudspeaker unit. Most high-quality loudspeaker units contain more than one speaker. A *tweeter* can reproduce high frequencies that other speakers cannot reach. So one is often used in conjunction with a standard loudspeaker to extend the frequency range reproduced. Sometimes, a *woofer*, designed to handle the lowest frequencies, is used with a mid-range *squawker* and a tweeter. A simple electronic circuit, called a crossover unit, ensures that the right signals go to each speaker.

A good loudspeaker unit connected to a cheap radio or record player will often give a startling improvement in sound quality. But you will also notice certain defects that were not apparent before. Your woofer may reveal that the amplifier produces considerable hum. Or your tweeter may show that it produces a lot of hiss. More likely than not, both faults will be present. Let's face it, you really do need a high quality amplifier. This is usually supplied as a separate item to which various sound sources can be connected. Most radios, record players and tape recorders have a socket so that you can connect a lead from them direct to your high quality amplifier. This arrangement should give a much better sound. But you will probably still find things to complain about. Record turntables tend to produce a disturbing rumble. Many tape recorders reproduce few treble signals, apart from hiss. And radio tuners are often highly susceptible to electrical interference from cars and other sources. Your high quality amplifier will emphasize all such defects. So you will end up having to spend yet more money in order to improve your sound system.

However much you improve the quality of your equipment,

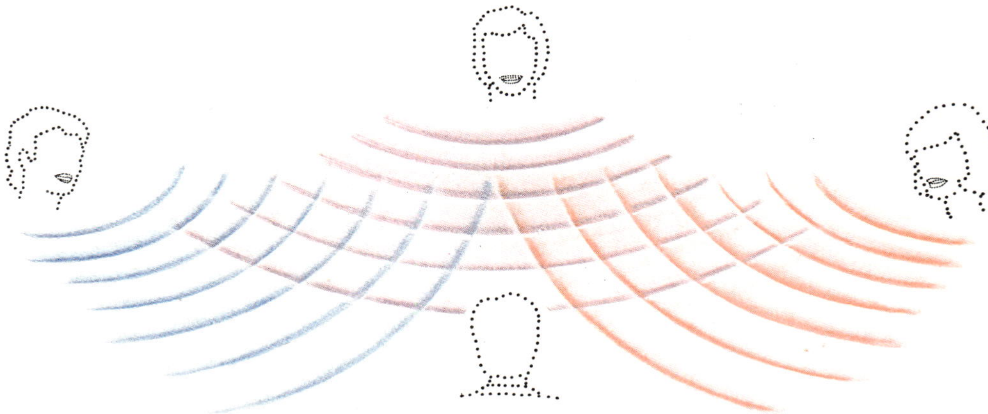

We judge the direction of sounds in two ways – by their timing and loudness. Sounds coming from in front of us reach both ears at the same time and with the same intensity. Sounds coming from one side reach one ear slightly before the other. And the sound in the closer ear will be slightly more intense. These subtle differences allow our brain to work out where the sounds are coming from. In a stereo system, slightly different signals fed to our ears give us the illusion of hearing sounds from various directions.

reproduction from a simple monophonics system can never sound completely natural. All the sound comes from one place, whereas sound normally comes to us from various directions. This problem can be partly overcome by installing a stereophonic sound system. The source supplies two separate sound signals that are amplified and fed to two separate loudspeaker units.

When a sound is made directly in front of us, the sound waves reaching each ear are of the same intensity (strength). Also, they are exactly in phase, or step, with each other. But, when a sound comes to us from one side, the nearest ear hears the sound slightly earlier than the other ear, and at a slightly higher intensity. These differences are detected by the brain and enable us to sense the direction from which the sound comes. This facility helps us to separate voices in a crowd. We can concentrate on what one person is saying, even if others are talking more loudly, as long as the sounds are coming from different directions. However, we cannot do the same with a monophonic tape recording of the sounds. We may be able to hear what the person nearest to the microphone was saying, but most of the voices will appear to be mixed up. For all the sound now comes from the same point. This is a problem that arises daily on radio programmes in which lively guests have an informal discussion. Often, several people talk at once. In the studio, the participants have no difficulty listening

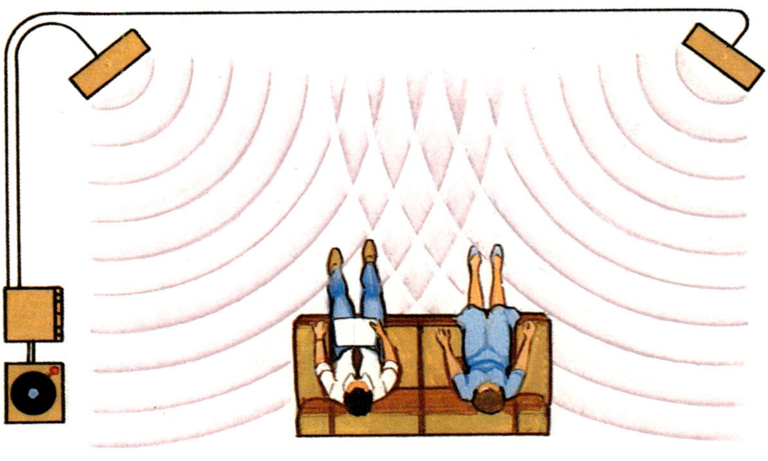

The pick-up converts the stereo signals of the record into electric signals. These are amplified separately and reproduced on a pair of loudspeaker units. To listeners in the area shown, the sounds seem to come from various positions between the two loudspeakers.

The sounds from two microphones are used to modulate (vary) a radio signal produced in the transmitter. The amplified signal is radiated by the transmitting aerial. Signals picked up by the receiving aerial are decoded in the tuner to form a pair of stereo signals. These are amplified and then reproduced on two loudspeakers to recreate the original spread of sound.

to one another. But, at home, with all the sounds coming from one loudspeaker, the listener has an almost impossible task in trying to hear what anyone is saying. If, however, the programme is broadcast and received in stereo, the problem disappears. In the studio, two microphones pick up signals similar to those that your ears would hear. At home, these signals are reproduced through separate loudspeakers. In this way, the ears receive sounds similar to those that would be heard in the studio. And subtle differences in intensity, phase or both make the various sounds appear to come from different directions. This is why there is no longer any difficulty in concentrating on one particular sound.

In any room, we hear sounds coming from all directions, not just in front of us. So, although a stereo system is a great improvement on a mono system, it cannot produce a completely realistic impression of the original sounds. However, the situation can be improved by using a quadraphonic (four-channel) system. With this, the listener has two loudspeakers behind him, as well as two in front. By feeding these four loudspeakers with appropriate signals, the listener can be surrounded by sound. He can, for example, be given the impression that he is sitting in a concert hall, with most of the sound coming from the front, and reverberation coming from the back and sides. This is the realistic approach to quadraphonic sound reproduction. Another technique is to give the listener the feeling that he is seated among the musicians. This can be done by recording an orchestra using four microphones in the middle. The violins might come from the left, the brass from the right, and other instruments from the front and back.

Although a quadraphonic system can surround us with sound, it does not give us any information about the height from which various sounds come. Some enthusiasts would like the sound image to be completed by having four additional channels to convey this information. However, few people would like to have eight loudspeakers, and their associated amplifiers and other equipment would be much more than the average person would want to pay. In fact, few people can be bothered to equip themselves with quadraphonic equipment. For, even if they had it, they would find relatively few quadraphonic recordings to play on it. The situation seems unlikely to change in the near future, so we shall concentrate here on the highly popular stereophonic sound systems.

Stereophonic Sound Systems

In order to enjoy stereophonic sound, you need two loudspeaker units and amplifiers and, of course, a source of stereo sound signals. In typical domestic equipment, the two amplifiers and their associated controls are usually combined in a single unit—the stereo amplifier. As in a mono system, this will have volume, treble and bass controls. Any one of these controls should have an equal effect on the two sound channels. If, for example, you turn up the volume control, this will increase the volume from both loudspeakers. One control not found on mono amplifiers is the balance control. This is a special form of volume control that increases the volume of one channel while decreasing the volume of the other. If the sound appears to come mostly from one side, the listener can adjust this control until a satisfactory balance, or spread of sound, is obtained. As with a mono amplifier, various sources, such as a radio tuner, record player or tape can be used.

Sound and Electronics

Since the development of the telephone in the 1860s, sound and electronics have been closely linked. In the telephone, a microphone changed sound waves into electrical signals. And, at the receiving end, an earpiece converted the signals back into sounds. In the early 1900s, the advent of the triode valve made it possible to amplify the signals. They could then be converted to high level sounds by means of a loudspeaker. The valve amplifier also enabled radio to develop from a Morse code signalling system into a medium for high-quality sound broadcasting. Techniques were devised for controlling the tone of the sounds produced, and these benefited the gramophone industry too. Another important feature of the amplifying valve was that it was capable of oscillation—that is, it could generate an electric signal. If its frequency was in the audible range, the signal could be converted into a sound. This made electronic music possible. An electronic organ could be made by having several oscillators, producing notes one semitone apart, operated by switches on a keyboard.

The transistor, developed in 1948, performs similar functions to the valve, but is much smaller and more reliable. With circuits using numerous valves, failures were frequent. But transistorised equipment performing the same functions would normally run for long periods without any trouble.

With an understanding of musical waveforms, circuits were designed to synthesise, or build up, similar waveforms from their separate harmonic components. In this way, the sound of any instrument could be simulated electronically. And new sounds, unlike those of any ordinary instrument, could be created too. Later, scientists started to design circuits that would imitate the complex sound patterns of the human voice. Each separate sound component in the words had to be generated at the appropriate time, with suitable pauses between the words. Products using this technology are now in everyday use.

Blind people, in particular, benefit from the talking clocks now available. Instead of displaying the time on hands, or as numbers, these clocks speak the time when a button is pressed. All the electronic components needed to generate the sound signals are contained in an integrated circuit—a microscopic circuit constructed on a chip of silicon.

Even more complex is the technique of electronic speech recognition. Humans learn to recognize many different accents, and can often guess correctly a word spoken indistinctly by considering the meaning of the other words with it. To design circuits that will do all this is proving a difficult task. However, simpler machines that can understand short commands consisting of only a few, clearly spoken words, are already in operation.

Offices and factories of the future will rely heavily on electronic voice recognition and synthesis techniques. Machines will carry out various tasks on command—unless their computer decides that the command is foolish or impossible. In such a case, the machine would then ask you questions in order to determine whether the command was acceptable. And, if you persisted in giving unsuitable commands, the machine might well have a quiet word with your boss!

Glossary

Acoustics The science of sound. Also, the effect that a room or object has on sound waves.

Amplitude Modulation (A.M.) Sound signals can be broadcast by using them to modulate (vary) the amplitude (strength) of radio waves. Electrical interference produces this modulation too. So the received signals suffer from background hiss and clicks.

Bass The lower sound frequencies. The bass control on a typical amplifier enables the output below about 1,000 hertz to be boosted or decreased.

Decibel (dB) A unit for comparing powers or sound intensity levels. The number of decibels difference is equal to 10 $\log_{10} P_1/P_2$, where P_1 and P_2 are the quantities being compared. If P_1 is twice P_2, then P_1 is 10 $\log_{10}2 = 3$ dB higher than P_2.

Dynamic Range The power ratio between strongest and weakest sounds. The dynamic range of a symphony orchestra can be as much as 90 decibels. The dynamic range of recorded sound is usually compressed. Low levels are increased to overcome background noise. And high levels are decreased to avoid distortion in amplifiers.

Frequency The rate at which waves or vibrations occur. A frequency of one hertz (Hz) is equal to one cycle (complete wave) per second One kilohertz (kHz) is equal to 1,000 hertz. The sound frequency range extends from about 20 Hz to 20 kHz.

Frequency Response The manner in which an amplifier, or other device, responds to signals of various frequencies. Frequency response is usually shown as a graph of output level against frequency. A perfect hi-fi amplifier would have a flat response—that is, it would respond equally to all sound frequencies.

Frequency Modulation (F.M.) Sound signals can be broadcast by using them to modulate (vary) the frequency (rate) of radio waves. In the radio receiver, the frequency variations are converted back into sounds. The receiver does not detect amplitude modulation caused by electrical interference. So the background noise is very low. This is one reason why F.M. receivers are used in high quality sound systems.

Hertz (Hz) A unit for measuring frequency. See FREQUENCY.

Loudness The loudness of a sound depends on its intensity (energy level) and the response of our ears. The latter varies with frequency, and makes bass sounds seem much quieter than mid-range sounds of the same intensity. This effect is most noticeable at low sound levels. So turning down an amplifier's volume control makes the bass sounds fade faster than the others. Some amplifiers have a loudness control, which compensates for this effect by applying some bass boost at low sound levels.

Major and Minor Scales The 8-note scale has two variations—the major scale and the minor scale. Starting with middle C on the piano and playing all the white notes up to the next C produces the scale of C major. This scale is formed by the following pattern: tone, tone, semitone, tone, tone, tone, semitone. By using this pattern, a major scale can be played, starting with any note on the keyboard. The minor scale has a characteristic sad sound. It too has its own pattern: the half tones occur between the second and third and between the fifth and sixth notes of the scale. This pattern will apply for all minor scales, starting on any note.

Pitch The pitch of a note—how shrill or deep it sounds—is determined mainly by its frequency. As the frequency of the vibrations increases, the pitch of the note increases too.

Quadraphonic Sound A system in which separate sound signals are reproduced on four loudspeakers surrounding the listener. This can give a good illusion of being in a concert hall, and is sometimes used to place the listener among the musicians.

Resonance When sound waves strike a body, they make it vibrate. The body is then said to be in *forced resonance.* At one particular frequency, the body will vibrate much more strongly. This is the body's *natural resonant frequency,* and the body is said to be *in resonance* at this frequency.

Stereophonic Sound A system in which separate sound signals are reproduced on two spaced loudspeakers, or fed to each side of a pair of headphones. Stereophonic sound gives the illusion that sounds are coming from various points in front of the listener.

Tone Colour The timbre, or quality of a musical note that distinguishes it from the same note played on a different instrument. The tone colour is determined by the harmonics produced by the instrument.

Treble The upper sound frequencies. An amplifier's treble control usually enables the output above about 1,000 hertz to be boosted or decreased.

Wavelength The physical length of one complete wave produced by a vibrating body. Sound wavelengths range from about 17 metres (low frequency) to about 17 millimetres (high frequency).

Wow and Flutter Variations in the pitch of a recorded note caused by speed variations in the recording or replay equipment. Pitch variations occurring at a rate of under 20 hertz are called wow. Faster variations are called flutter.

Index

Page numbers in *italics* refer to illustrations.

ACKNOWLEDGEMENTS
Cover Roger Phillips by kind permission of Studio Sound. Title & Contents De Monde Advertising. Pages 8 & 10 Paul Brierley. 11 Allsport. 12 R.A.E. Farnborough. 13 Zefa. 15 top right Science Photo Library, bottom John Watney. 16 Paul Brierley. 22 & 25 Sonia Halliday. 26 Leyland Vehicles. 28 Richard Bryant. 29 Bruel & Kjaer. 35 & 36 Edison National Historic Site. 37 top Michael Holford, bottom Science Museum. 38 Michael Holford. 39 Hamlyn Picture Library. 40-42 Hulton Picture Library. 44 Paul Brierley. 45 EMI. 46 top David Redfurn. 46 & 47 EMI. 50 top left Paul Brierley, top right, centre & bottom EMI Tapes. 52 Paul Brierley. Back cover Edison Historical Site.

Picture research Penny Warn